Reflections

Reflections

Living in God's Daily Presence

2012

Witherspoon
PRESS
Louisville, Kentucky

Contributors: Julia Boyce, Katrina Pekich Bundy, Suzy Edwards, Barry Ensign-George, Sarah Erickson, David Gambrell, Lee Hinson-Hasty, Cathy Hoop, Melissa Kirkpatrick, Ann Knox, Elizabeth Lovell, Krista Lovell, Diane Karay Myers, Rose Niles, Kevin Park, Karen Russell, Teresa Stricklen, Billie Sutter, Jill Tolbert, Janet Tuck, Tammy Wiens, Betsy Wiley, Charles Wiley, Susan Wisseman

Reflections: Living in God's Daily Presence is based on *Home Daily Bible Readings,* copyright © 2008 by the Committee on the Uniform Series, and uses the New Revised Standard Version of the Bible, copyright © 1989 by the Division of Christian Education of the National Council of the Churches of Christ in the United States of America. Both used by permission.

For information or a complete listing of resources, contact Congregational Ministries Publishing, Presbyterian Church (U.S.A.), 100 Witherspoon Street, Louisville, KY 40202-1396.

Every effort has been made to trace copyrights on the materials included in this book. If any copyrighted material has nevertheless been included without permission and due acknowledgment, proper credit will be inserted in future printings after notice has been received.

Published by Witherspoon Press, a ministry of the General Assembly Mission Council, Presbyterian Church (U.S.A.), Louisville, Kentucky.

Website address: pcusa.org/witherspoon

ISBN 9781571532138

Contents

*W*elcome to *Reflections: Living in God's Daily Presence,* 365 readings that will encourage you. These devotions are sure to inspire moments of contemplation on and celebration of God's purpose for you, while guiding you through your day.

Each reading is based on the Cooperative Uniform Lesson Series of Scripture readings. *Reflections* is the perfect companion to your study of the Bible, whether you use *The Present Word* or any other study based on the series.

Beginning with January 1, the daily readings take you through the seasons of 2012. Make time during winter, spring, summer, and fall to pause and consider the word of God. Turn to *Reflections* to give substance to your spiritual disciplines through the year.

Reflections is a spiritual breather for those longing for a deeper relationship with God. I hope you will find refreshment for your soul and fodder for your faith.

Mark D. Hinds,
Editor

Begin with a brief silence.

Breathe.

Pray for the Holy Spirit's leading.

Read the Scripture passage.

Focus on a word or phrase that speaks to you.

Breathe.

Read the daily devotion.

Look and listen for ways the readings confirm or challenge your faith.

Thank God.

A Warm Retreat from the Cold and Gray

*P*otiphar's wife is a royal pain. She is the lawbreaker, ridiculous and dangerous, waving Joseph's garment in the air. She is abusive; Joseph is the victim. He could have avoided the fiasco if he had turned around once he realized that he would be alone with his boss's wife. Just as in his boyhood, Joseph shows himself to be naïve; again, he will pay a heavy price.

We can be innocent and naïve, unaware of the emotional and physical dangers abusive people can inflict. Abusers can have no idea they are hurting someone. Victims can be like the proverbial frog in the pot of water, unaware until the situation is dire. Emotional abuse is more subtle than physical abuse and can be more devastating. Unfortunately, people like Potiphar's wife can go a lifetime without encountering truth tellers who lead them to examine their behaviors, to repent, and to ask forgiveness.

This episode is part of the evil perpetrated against Joseph that God uses for providential purposes. God is with victims of abuse. God repeatedly calls abusers to become conscious and stop causing others pain. Avoid the company of people who cause you pain, and pray that they wake from their sin.

Loving God, guide me today that I may not cause another pain. May my words bring others peace, and may my actions speak of love; in Jesus' name. Amen.

Some of the wisest people I have ever known were not professional counselors but fellow students or friends, sometimes strangers. Joseph's fellow prison inmates didn't need professional dream interpreters; they needed one person to be a channel of divine guidance.

God gives a gift to every soul. Some are best nourished in technical school, college, or seminary; others need only life experience and the guidance of the Holy Spirit. A person's gift is usually clear to others and becomes clear to oneself over time.

Joseph's ability to interpret dreams was God-given and eventually led to many people being saved from starvation. One of my neighbors had a superb gift of hospitality, making others feel welcome. Another hungered for justice and placed herself in harm's way to witness for peace in Iraq. Some have gifts of patience, of humor, or of understanding the way things work.

God distributes gifts so that our needs and others' abilities mesh in providential time. Joseph volunteered his gift to others. Will you offer yours? You may be the only person in a position to interpret an event or a dream; to understand a person; or to bestow a smile, an embrace, or a loving word.

God, give me wisdom to recognize my gift, boldness to use it, and humility to acknowledge you as the giver; through Christ our Lord. Amen.

*H*ope deferred makes the heart sick," says Proverbs 13:12, "but a desire fulfilled is a tree of life." Pharaoh's cupbearer confides a dream to Joseph and discovers he will soon be released from prison. Joseph's hope for release will be deferred; the butler will forget all about him when he is invited to party with Pharaoh.

The rest of the world may party the night away. Laughter and music may spill out the windows. It is hard to be left out; harder yet to be forgotten.

When I lived in England, so far from all I had known, it was an exile for my heart. I did not know when I would be able return home. No one knew me there. One day a gypsy came to the door. She wanted me to buy the shawl she held in her hands, but I wasn't interested. Then she volunteered, "You will fly away on two wings." We left England two years later.

The Spirit says, "Endure." The Spirit says, "Hope." Christ remembers you and knows where you are; release will come. You are not forgotten; your name is written on the palm of God's hand.

God, when I am all alone, remember me. When no one speaks my name, remember me. Deliver me, and set me free; through Christ my Lord. Amen.

*T*he Spirit has given Joseph the gift of discerning meaning from mysterious images. Joseph is unable or unwilling to conceal what God reveals. Is he simply unable to control his mouth? Maybe. It would have been disastrous for the nation, though, if Joseph had decided to keep all his ideas to himself.

One summer afternoon I watched a neighbor mowing his yard on a noisy rider mower with a young boy on his lap. I became increasingly uncomfortable. Something urged me to go over. I resisted. The nudge became more insistent, and again I resisted. Finally, I approached. I gently told him that the little boy's hearing could be injured by the loud noise. He thanked me and took the boy inside the house.

Several months later, the boy's grandmother told me that the child, "Tom," went to a prayer meeting and asked the pastor to pray for his ears. Mother and grandmother were interested but did not know what to think. One afternoon, as a train whistled, Tom covered his ears, exclaiming that they hurt. "It looks like his hearing was damaged, and now he seems healed," she said, smiling at me. "Thank you! Do you know how hard it was for me to come over?" I replied.

Recognize a prompt of the Holy Spirit by the fruit that stems from obedience.

Holy Spirit, be a witness to truth within my heart, and give me courage to accept your direction through Jesus Christ. Amen.

5

*R*emember me; get me outta here!" Does the cupbearer remember Joseph's plea? No, his memory fades about the same time as Pharaoh's birthday party gets in high gear. They're "walking like Egyptians," and the dates are delicious. Nothing rivets you in the present like good company and food. "Send me a reminder," says a good friend, "I need to be reminded of our visits!" Should I mail her an appointment notice? Memories slip. The cupbearer's memory regains its footing two years later.

My sister Liz and I shared a bedroom when we were young. Before wishing me good night from the lower bunk, she sometimes asked me to remember something and tell her in the morning. I always remembered. What things did she ask me to recall? I forget.

Snow is on the ground; it is cold. Creatures have gone underground for a long sleep. Cold winds send us inside. Memories can enter a deep freeze due to age, illness, alcoholism. Yet God remembers and holds all that is precious to us in store.

Joseph dreams of freedom; months and years pass. God is with him—the refrain of his life (and ours). People may forget us; our names may slip from their tongues. "Forget me not!" I never will, says God.

Light of my heart, you know all that I am, and you love me with all that you are. I know you will never forget me; this gives joy to my soul; through Christ. Amen.

$\mathcal{P}$haraoh had two dreams: one of thin cows devouring fat cows, another of thin ears of corn swallowing plump ones. He held a national dream summit, but no one could interpret them.

As the magicians shuffle out the doors, the chief butler remembers Joseph. At this point, Pharaoh might have smacked his head and said, "I put this man in prison? Release him!"

Lies put Joseph in prison, but truth set him free. Prison has not changed him: he is forever a devout and modest man. God's touch makes one humble. Those given spiritual gifts know that they are instruments through which God works.

I once heard an operatic soprano sing during worship. She was technically superb, but I could scarcely listen because her attitude blazed like a banner across the sanctuary: "I'm so special! I'm extremely talented!" She made melody to herself, not God.

Joseph got out of the way, and God went to work. Ponder this when all eyes are on you: Will you trumpet yourself or be an instrument of the divine? If you are grounded in God, people will listen.

Merciful God, all good gifts come from you. Help me to acknowledge your presence in everything I do, that your will may be done; through Jesus Christ. Amen.

*E*very spring the Emergency Alert System tests tornado sirens. Select a safe shelter away from windows, they advise; stock it with food and water. When I was ten, my mother said the sky turned green on Palm Sunday afternoon. My fifth-grade teacher's house was hit by a tornado as the family fled in their car. Our class went on a salvage operation; there was nothing left.

"Be prepared," advises the Scouting motto. For what? Everything. Joseph receives emergency alerts from another source: harvest grain, the dreams told him; set a portion aside. Haul grain to the cities; treat the cats well.

God sends us guidance more frequently than we are aware. Our "reality" encompasses the spiritual as well as the natural world. Noah followed spiritual perceptions, as did Joseph of Egypt and Joseph of Nazareth.

God readies us for all that is to come by our thoughts and dreams, word of mouth and Scripture, and the groundwork of the Holy Spirit. All your needs will be met by Love that foresees all.

God of all dreamers, illumine my heart with your Holy Spirit that your truth may clearly shine within; through Christ my Lord. Amen.

*T*hose who humble themselves will be exalted," said Jesus. Joseph occupied the lowest place as a prison inmate; now he chairs Egypt's Agriculture Department and more. As in Jesus' parable about the dinner guests, Pharaoh says to Joseph, "Friend, move up higher" (Luke 14:10–11). The bowing-down business he dreamed about as a teenager has happened sooner than expected (Genesis 37:7, 9). From pit to palace, naïve youth to confidant of Pharaoh, Joseph is the ultimate rags-to-riches poster boy.

Jesus preached about a pearl of great price, about a mustard seed growing into a great shrub. A pinch of yeast, grains of wheat—tiny things with potential.

Because of what he has endured, Joseph has wisdom and discernment. He's had much time to pray, to reflect on the people he's met. He bears fruits of the Spirit: self-control, gentleness, faithfulness, kindness, patience, and peace (Galatians 5:22–23). He started out despised by his brothers, but now he's a member of the family of the Egyptian court. Above all, God is with him; Joseph has gentled himself to the work of the Spirit.

Most of us will never wear luxury clothes or bend our necks to accept a gold chain from a queen, king, or president. Yet if we humble ourselves and become like children, God will confer the greatest honor.

Blessed God, I bow my soul to you, for you have lifted me up and crowned me with the glory of my Savior. Amen.

$\mathcal{J}$oseph's brothers are sitting around staring at one another. "Why are you looking at one another?" their father finally demands. "Get off your duffs, and go get us some grain in Egypt so we don't all starve to death!"

"Do not associate with hotheads," warns a proverb (Proverbs 22:24b). Joseph has been at a distance from the brothers who sold him like a sack of potatoes, but that is about to change.

Hotheads are the ones who lead police officers on high-speed chases. They tail our cars at a distance of several yards and try to run us off roads. One blinded me at night by turning on megawatt lights a yard behind me. Today's hostile hotheads are tomorrow's desperate ones, dependent on the mercy of others.

To treat these "enemies" as anything other than children of God would be to reveal the famine in our hearts and admit spiritual starvation. Those who treat us poorly conceal great pain. Bless them, and be patient. They are making their way to God. They have made detours and gone off on wild joy rides, yet their longed-for destination is the same as ours.

Our one God awaits us all at the doorway of Love's eternal home.

O my God, give me understanding, that I may be gentle with those who treat me harshly; and give them grace to call upon you; through Jesus Christ our Lord. Amen.

$\mathcal{J}$oseph's dreams have come true: He is at the summit of power. His brothers pretended he was dead, now they look to him for life. He thirsted for water, now they hunger for bread. They could not "speak peaceably to him" before (Genesis 37:4); now his voice is harsh. He plans to test them to learn the truth about Benjamin and purify their hearts of the evil they have done. "We are honest men," they plea; Joseph stares at them with a blank face and puts them in prison.

Joseph's brothers have told him that he does not exist. What would you do if a sibling said to your face that you had passed away? Many of us would cut all ties. Joseph gives them a quiet room to ponder their actions.

God is with Joseph, helping him subdue any impulse to retaliation: not "an eye for an eye" but overcoming evil with good (Romans 12:21). If it depends on Joseph, he will "live peaceably with all" (12:18). His is the way of a brave soul, not a coward.

Do you love God? Then you know there are no strangers, just sisters and brothers you have yet to recognize. With God, cycles of vengeance and violence can be broken, and peace can take their place.

God, help me see to the soul of things, discerning your truth, reading your presence in the hearts of all; through Jesus Christ, my Redeemer. Amen.

*J*oseph's brothers would not listen to his pleas in the wilderness; now they listen to him in prison. He was their captive; now they are his. All the anguish they inflicted on him comes back to roost in their hearts. "The measure you give will be the measure you get back," said Jesus; "Do to others as you would have them do to you" (Luke 6:38, 31). Now the brothers know this to be true.

"We would not listen," they say to one another in shock. They were so intent on punishing the favorite son that they lost sight of his humanity.

A person who listens is an oasis of peace to others. The listener helps bring to awareness emotions that need to be felt and tears that must be shed in order to heal. Give others the gift of listening with the heart, and peace will flow back to you.

Indwelling God, you listen to me, and I am confident I am heard. Your peace reaches into me, soothing worries, bringing joy. Thank you for your healing presence through Christ Jesus. Amen.

I am bereaved of my children, I am bereaved," laments Jacob (v. 14). Losing one son sent him into grief; the thought of losing another deepens his pain. Judah offers to bear the blame if anything goes wrong. Previously, the brothers cared nothing for their father's feelings, lying to his face about Joseph's fate.

"Not my problem" is a common phrase, often said with a grin. We are responsible for so much that it is a relief when something is outside our jurisdiction. Yet we look up to those who offer to shoulder blame or help others in troubled situations.

Jesus could have walked by the sick and the troubled, but he stopped and helped. He stopped for us, too, when he shouldered the cross on which he would meet his death. "My problem," said his actions. "I lay down my life for you."

I was in the parsonage when a faulty electric circuit exploded down the lane, and it set the whole church on fire. I sped to the church to open the front doors for the firefighters, but I found melting metal. A passing motorist drove into the parking lot and told me to get away from the building.

When I returned to the scene later, the sidewalk where I had stood was covered with shattered glass. I could have been impaled were it not for a stranger.

Merciful God, thank you for the kindness of strangers, the care of family, and your guardian love; in Jesus' name. Amen.

*O*nce someone has broken your trust with a lie, betrayal, or uncivil behavior, it can be nearly impossible for him or her to gain it back. Emotional wounds mark the psyche. Joseph has been afflicted, and we cannot fault him for being reluctant to trust again. Naïve as a youth, he is now astute and wise.

Several people betrayed my trust and now have passed away. One never apologized for her behavior; I think they all scarcely knew what they were doing. I am not as naïve as once I was, but wise? Not yet. How can I protect myself? I place my trust in God.

For years, I had a Mennonite doctor. His wife came to my rescue when I injured my fingers. He told me that he and she met when they were both praying for direction in love. I mentioned this to someone recently, and he scoffed. I did the same and met a prayerful man with whom I have much in common; we are often startled with joy.

Give God your heart, and God will soothe it; your emptiness, and God will fill it; your grief, and God will ease it; your mistrust, and God will bring you peace.

God, you know the needs I conceal, my fears, my desires, and my hopes. Give me grace to trust you like a child, confident of your love through Christ my Lord. Amen.

The Scripture for today is from Judah's speech to Joseph, pleading for release of Benjamin that he might take his place as a slave. Joseph has been longing to hear this: evidence that they will not leave behind another brother and break their father's heart yet again. Judah's words in verse 16, "God has found out the guilt of your servants," also imply that the brothers acknowledge the guilt for their criminal treatment of Joseph. Joseph's repeated testing of his brothers brought them to repentance. One victim has changed the hearts of those who violated him.

Our culture does not thirst for the rehabilitation of criminals but rather for justice, and that usually means prison time. Detective shows and murder mysteries grip our imaginations. We feel satisfaction as the prison door clangs shut on another case.

Our opinions about the convicted are very distant from Jesus' teaching. Therefore, we should not be surprised when the Holy Spirit bridges the chaotic realm between our fears and the needs of those who have been brought to searing recognition of their guilt.

God may test our hearts, searching for repentance, forgiveness, and love. Dare we give God further cause for sorrow?

Merciful God, who searches for those who have lost their way, do not let me hinder or discourage anyone who seeks redemption in Jesus Christ our Lord. Amen.

Surely the LORD is in this place—and I did not know it!"
Jacob once declared (Genesis 28:16). Now his sons can make
the words their own.

"Don't beat yourselves up over this," Joseph says to them.
"You blame yourselves, but God wanted me here." The brothers
had no clue as they smoldered at his gliding around in his
fancy coat, threw him in a pit, and sold him to passing traders.
They did not recognize Joseph as they visited Egypt for grain.
They had no idea God's hand was deftly at work.

In high school physics, I had a difficult time grasping the
concept of atoms. Atoms were intangible; I could not see them.
I found God incomprehensible too and asked, "Are you a
personal or impersonal God?" I received an immediate answer:
the marked impression that I would find out in due time.

I have found God at work through dogged days at a desk;
as sorrow made itself at home, while I made pan after pan of
grapefruit gelatin; and as a stranger shouted, "Get away from
the building!" God has made signboards of my dreams and
messengers of my friends; I am in awe.

One day God will stand revealed, and we will weep for joy.

*Holy God, you hold all things in your hands and are surely with
me through Christ. I say, "Amen" and "Thank you!"*

I have never lived anywhere more than six years since I was eighteen. It takes me about two years to settle in. I am tired of being uprooted, weary of short-lived friendships and immature gardens.

My widowed mother moved from her home to a retirement dwelling. Community workers mowed the yard and took care of the snow. She made many new friends. Some who would benefit from smaller quarters and more safeguards find it difficult to contemplate relocation. Transplanting is easier if one is young, but roots grow strong over the years.

My mother was an intuitive person whose "gut" told her when it was the right time to move. None of her daughters needed to raise the issue.

It may take time for us to recognize God's providence in things outside our control. Joseph swept away the veil from his brother's eyes, and now it is Jacob's turn: confirmation of God's will comes in a dream.

God never leaves us without guidance. The more surprising and difficult the passage we face, the more clearly does God say, "Do not be afraid; I am here."

God, in Jesus you moved from place to place with nowhere to lay your head. You understand our longing for home. Help us to take root in you that we may always be at peace; through Christ. Amen.

*F*ather and son are powerfully reunited, and tears flow. After the reunion, practical considerations command the family's attention. There are animals to feed, luggage to unpack, and plans to make for meeting with Pharaoh.

Joseph does not tattle on his brothers nor recount the humiliation of being sold as a slave and thrown in prison. He does not brag about his dream-interpreting skills or his rise to power. Jacob does not moan about his grief and sleepless nights. They are present to each other; the past "is finished and gone."

Not much can be gained by clinging to the past. We must live in the present and look forward. Jesus asks us to follow him; there is no time to linger and look back. Jesus did not say, "Remember grudges; keep old wounds raw; worry about what you could have done differently." He speaks in the present tense: "Stand up"; "Little girl, get up!" (Mark 2:11; 5:41); "Be merciful. . . . Do not judge. . . . Forgive" (Luke 6:36, 37); "Feed my sheep" (John 21:17).

God has more to give us: there is more joy and meaning, more laughter and light yet to be revealed. The Holy Spirit refreshes every heart and the face of the earth.

Loving God, you call me to leave behind all that interrupts communion with you. Give me courage to step out on your word, knowing you are with me; through Christ my Savior. Amen.

*W*hy don't you buy a white car," my mother suggested as we stood in the car lot. She could get me an employee discount. "I don't want a white car," I replied. "It blinds me." A few years later, she purchased a white car and then complained it was too bright. Our relationship had been like this since my childhood. She assumed I liked canned peaches and banana bread, but these were my sisters' preferences. She never realized I preferred fresh peaches and date bread.

In 2008, she was diagnosed with late-stage ovarian cancer. In the spring of 2009, she moved to my sister's home for hospice care. I drove to Ohio for my final visit. After several days, I talked with my mother for the last time. She asked me to pray with her, and then I told her all that I knew of heaven, gathering together Jesus' promises and the wisdom of Revelation. Joy settled within us, and tears spilled from our eyes. She saw a tear on the edge of my nose, extended her hand, took my tear, and pressed it to her lips. This was her blessing, a gift sought for years.

Pain or joy may be our heritage, but we can choose to bless those we love during the years we live together. Life is short; joy gives us heaven on earth.

God, my joy, grant me a loving heart and forgiving spirit that I may be kind to others as the day is long and be at peace when my years come to an end; through Jesus Christ. Amen.

I drive with the flow of traffic, not speeding to get to the next stop light first nor holding others up. Yet on every journey, it seems, there is a vehicle far too close, impatient. When they pass, I don't want to see a window rolling down.

Recently I read a man's T-shirt: "If you're not a hunter, I don't even want to see you." I didn't want him to see me either: his message made me uneasy. Words can alienate and wound or befriend and heal.

I worked as a pastoral intern one summer at a hospital for the mentally ill in Washington, D.C. I approached one man who didn't meet my eyes, extend his hand, or utter a word. He locked his sorrow deep within. I knew not to underestimate the power of attentive presence, so I stayed with him a while. Before I left, I said, "God bless you," with warmth. I didn't expect a response, and then I saw a large tear fall from the corner of his eye.

As the world becomes more anxious and impatient, we can radiate warmth and kindness to others, blessing them (at least through silent prayer) as Jacob blessed Joseph: "God will help you; God will bless you."

Shepherd God, restrain my tongue from unkind words, my mind from mean thoughts, and my hands from hurtful actions. Heal my memories and emotions through Jesus Christ. Amen.

*I*n a meadow in Wales, I saw an ancient burial chamber. Sheep grazed nearby. Dew glistened on grass under the soft morning sun. I glanced inside but saw only fallen chips of stone and dirt.

Jacob tells his children to place his remains in the cave in Canaan where his parents and grandparents were buried. They will honor their father's final wish.

When we take our last breath, we are on the threshold of Christ the Door, who has prepared a place for us. He reassures us that we need not fear.

When I was about nine years old, I woke in the night abruptly with the knowledge that my parents would be gone one day and I would be all alone. Now they have both passed, but I know I am not orphaned. God is with me and with you.

On this earth, Jesus will give peace to all who ask, and afterward he will take away all tears and pain as he guides us into the presence of infinite Love. Our souls will shine with joy.

Holy God, bless those who are grieving now, and let your peace rest about their shoulders. I thank you for their lives, their love to me and faith in you; through Christ our Lord. Amen.

$\mathcal{M}$y father died in early September on a perfect summer day. In the funeral home, I stood near his body and apologized for everything I'd ever done that might have caused him pain. This included breaking a wood cornice he'd built, a child's perceived "sin" he forgave years before. I was startled when he interrupted my confession with the inner words "I am not here; I am risen." I wiped away my tears and moved to let another pay her respects.

His death struck me hard. "How do people endure this?" I asked a friend, stunned to realize that there were others bearing such sorrow.

My grandfather died in a traffic accident while following the hearse carrying the body of an employee. When I see a line of cars following a hearse, I pull to the curb and pray. Their procession is linked with the company of mourners who followed my grandfather's body. In a far deeper sense we are all spiritually connected, united in Christ's mystical Body.

"Rejoice with those who rejoice," counsels Paul, and "weep with those who weep" (Romans 12:15). We do this until God wipes away all of our tears.

Light of heaven, you promise a time when death will be no more. Until that day, comfort me in sorrow and support me when I cannot stand, through the grace of Christ our Lord. Amen.

*O*ne summer my parents took the family on a vacation to the Rocky Mountains. Cooked outside and eaten at a mountain table, canned chicken and potatoes tasted better than fresh. We returned home and school began.

"Write a one-page report about your summer," said the teacher. I had much to tell, especially about how our father had saved our lives on "Going to the Sun Road." My teacher commented, "Diane, some day you will write a book." The words stayed with me. I was quiet at home but vocal on paper. One day, I wrote a book of prayers.

I have often wished I were a more agile talker, but decades of forced listening and my own inclination channeled my voice into writing. From time to time, someone thanks me for giving voice to their prayers, prayers they had no words to express. God worked through my burden to give others words to praise, confess, and intercede.

Can you see how God is working for good through your trials? Carry your cross with patience: God will bless you with peace for all that you have endured.

Savior God, you are always working to bring blessing out of trial. I give you thanks for your mercy through Jesus Christ. Amen.

*B*ereavement knocks us off balance and drags us into an ocean of tears. Joseph must have felt this way when he was hurled into the pit and thrown into prison. Jacob too was helpless before a torn and bloodied robe.

In the first weeks after my husband's death, I was terrified of being poor and having nowhere to go. There was no way out but by plunging into the chaos. The psalmist tells us that God works in the midst of the storms and churning waters: "Your way was through the sea, your path, through mighty waters" (v. 19). God does not give us a way to escape the storms that beset us but accompanies us through them.

I visited Pensacola beach in Florida on my first vacation in years. I was a new widow; a cousin snapped a picture of me alone in the water. As I walked along the shore, saltwater erased my footprints.

I have made my way into a new life I could not have imagined several years ago. All of the difficulties have been solved, a financial path found, a new home made in another city. We cannot see God's footprints on the shores we walk alone. Yet when tears are past, we will know God was with us in the midst of the storm.

Holy God, hold up those who struggle against overwhelming currents, and bring them to the calm shores of your love; through Jesus Christ. Amen.

*L*aughing Abraham and Sarah bore Isaac; Isaac bore Jacob; and Jacob, twelve sons, each who had children. God has been faithful to the promise made to Abraham, to become great and mighty (Genesis 18:18). Abraham became a nomad; Jacob and his children, immigrants; now their descendents have become a numerous and powerful people settled in Egypt. Stories of family conflict yield to the narrative of the Israelites, God's chosen people.

As the Israelites grew numerous, their faith also grew strong: "Our steps are made firm by the LORD . . . for the LORD holds us by the hand" (Psalm 37:23–24). Israel's greatest strength is not prolific childbearing but faith. Without faith, their great numbers would mean little.

Our richness in life is not in the quantity of our possessions, the size of our home, or ample bank accounts and investments. God's blessing is not shown in the number of children we have or do not have. Many families are large but do not raise kind and just children.

Money cannot purchase treasure in heaven. Children cannot make us right with God. We are rich when it is well with our souls.

Delight of my heart, lead me this day in love, and tonight, let me lie down in peace; through Christ, my Savior. Amen.

A new pharaoh has taken power in Egypt and perceives
a threat where none exists: what if this people continue to
grow rapidly, and a war begins, and they join forces with our
enemies and decide to fight us and take flight? This daydream
will have dire consequences for the Israelites.

Much comedy uses hypothetical situations to set the stage for
humorous outcomes. My mother told me that she once feared
her four daughters would become teenagers wearing high heels
and flaming red lipstick. She was surprised that we wore flat
"hippie" shoes and no lipstick.

Much tragedy also ensues from daydreams gone badly.
Because of Pharaoh's paranoid thoughts, the Israelites will
be forced to endure harsh forced labor and will grow bitter
with despair.

When we have fearful daydreams, we would be wise to draw
our thoughts into the present. This will prevent worries from
settling in for a long duration and perhaps make others' lives
much easier.

*Shepherd God, call me away from my daydreams and my fears
that I may be fully present to you and your beloved people;
through Christ my Lord. Amen.*

The king of Egypt is threatened by babies. He orders two midwives to appear and recruits them as special agents. Maybe he barked an order and took the women's silence as cooperation. If so, he was wrong. The midwives deliver life into the world; it is not their nature to kill. Shiphrah and Puah ignore the edict because they answer to a higher power. More babies are born, and the Israelite community continues to grow.

The women are summoned to appear in the royal court. "Why have you allowed the boys to live?" Pharaoh snarls. The women begin the course toward liberation of the Hebrews, later taken up by more women: Moses' mother and sister and the daughter of Pharaoh, who will save Moses' life. Meanwhile, Pharaoh realizes he has been duped. He enlists the entire country in his genocidal plan. Shiphrah and Puah fear God. God guides their conscience and fills them with revulsion at Pharaoh's suggestion.

The world may pressure us to conspire against others and to act in a vindictive or unkind manner. In Christ, we have the freedom to disobey, for God alone is Lord of the conscience.

Do not submit to demands of those who contradict the voice of love.

Merciful God, guide me and guard me this day, that I may act in love, with wisdom, and under the protection of Christ my Lord. Amen.

I was walking around a city square in England when I heard shouts. Looking up, I saw two men slugging each other. Horrified, I diverted my eyes and quickened my pace, suddenly finding myself near a weeping boy, perhaps nine years old. I guessed he was the son of one of the fighters. I folded my arm around him and diverted his gaze away from the scene. A shopkeeper called the police. They arrived quickly and separated the men. The boy ran to his father, who drew him to his side.

Moses witnessed the intense suffering of his people but felt inadequate to take on a tyrant. Moses was right, yet this weakness enabled God to work through him. Moses guided the people to the edge of the sea, then God cast Pharaoh's army down like a stone.

There are many people who need to be rescued, saved from themselves, saved from cruel circumstances and from others. Be like Moses. Do as much as you can do, however inadequate you feel, that God may work powerfully and for great good.

Eternal God, help me to leave behind all excuses and feelings of low worth that I may be an open channel for your peace; in Jesus' name. Amen.

*W*ho is like God among the gods? There is only one God, true light shining in human souls. This Holy One called Abraham, wrestled with Jacob, watched over Joseph, reassured Moses, swallowed up Pharaoh's army, and delivered a people from slavery.

Contemporary entertainment culture and advertising offer mortals chances to become idols, stars, even goddesses. But God does not shave; cares not for idol status, molten or vocal; and is unimpressed by celebrity status.

We do not often notice God acting on a grand scale, yet this is scarcely an invitation to build egos and empires in a quest to become godlike. Stars may "reign" for several decades; God reigns forever. "Idols" create a fan base, not reverence. All our heroes, champions, stars, and idols are simply one with all humanity, flourishing for a day, swept away tomorrow like withered grass.

Only God endures forever, together with the souls of those who accept divine love as their abiding place. Our holy God is worthy of our deepest reverence and calls us to love one another from the heart.

God, you seek humble hearts, open minds, and willing hands. Help me place you first, that I may receive all else as gift through Christ my Lord. Amen.

The people of Israel complain. In response, God asks two simple things: "Listen to my voice" and "Do what is right." But the murmuring is just beginning, and God will sigh, "O Israel, if you would but listen to me!" (Psalm 81:8). The people will also fail to listen to Moses (Exodus 16:20) and consequently will find worms, not manna, for breakfast one morning.

Few of us are good listeners. We must work hard to give others our full attention. When we can, it is an oasis of peace in a culture of interruptions and inattention.

How much more difficult it is to listen to God. No wonder God grumbles, "O that my people would listen to me, that Israel would walk in my ways!" (Psalm 81:13) Why does God desire our attention and obedience? To heal us.

When we are still and attentive in God's presence, God is joyful. The Holy Spirit searches over the rubble in our hearts and begins to cleanse, purify, and heal us.

When we listen well to others, it is healing for them. May God give us attentive hearts that others may be at peace.

God, quiet my inner clamor that I may hear your voice; through Christ my Savior. Amen.

*W*hen my parents visited Greece, they brought home an icon of Christ. Standing before this painting, focusing on Christ's eyes, I feel him gazing at me with holy intensity. Everywhere and always, God beholds us.

I took swimming lessons at the YMCA on Saturday mornings when I was young. Once when the rest of us were standing near the deep end, my friend Sam dove in and disappeared under the surface. He popped up a bit later at the shallow end, having swum the entire distance on one breath.

We cannot take a breather from God, disappear from God's attention, to reappear when it suits us. "Where can I flee from your presence?" (Psalm 139:7b). Why should we want to?

God is our salvation, rescuing us from our mistakes and sin; our refuge from danger; our comfort when tears fall; Living water, Vine, and Bread to nourish us in all our ways; Father, Son and Holy Spirit, who uphold us in joyful love.

"I walk before the Lord," says Psalm 116:9. It is our glory and comfort to live in the presence of the divine and tread a sacred path.

Savior God, guide my feet that I may not turn away from you but steadily progress into the joy of your presence; through Christ our Lord. Amen.

Tuesday, January 31
Romans 3:21–26

*I*n northern Indiana, winter can be treacherous. Summer driver's education classes didn't cover winter driving, so one January day my mother taught me how to drive on icy roads. She located a stretch of road free of telephone poles and ditches. "Get up to thirty miles an hour," she instructed. I sped up. "Now, brake hard." I did. The Barracuda went into a skid. When I lifted my foot off the brake, the car righted itself.

Scripture hints at the hazards we face when apart from divine love: instability, like a house built on sand; or unsound judgment due to lack of self-knowledge (Matthew 7:24–27; 7:1–5). Most of us need to experience these hazards firsthand in order to learn. Yet we are like infants behind the wheel. We need Jesus' instruction.

God knows that sin can freeze over the soul. Jesus took on himself the hazards of sin carried to their extremes so that we, fully trusting in him, would be spared the consequences. If we trust our Lord, we will not slide off the path he has chosen for us.

Scripture reading will not help us unless it leads us into a personal relationship with the divine. This friendship with our Savior sets us on the "glory road," our lifelong progression into the presence of the Holy.

God, bring me to such peace in knowing you that I may live in love, not fear, and joyfully serve you; through Jesus Christ. Amen.

Jesus did not preach of kings and queens, political leaders, or rags-to-riches merchants. He advised the exalted to humble themselves and made role models of unassuming children, a devout woman whose name history forgot, and a man who threw propriety to the wind as he climbed a tree to get a better view. He sought out the sick, the paralyzed, and the hopeless, not the arrogant, top-heavy with self-importance like bobble-head dolls. These came to him but went away grumbling at his demands.

I once dreamed of Jesus the janitor: a voice said that he would clean the room of a poor person but not that of a rich one. Jesus will clean our souls. All we have to do is admit our poverty, acknowledge our mess, and ask for help.

The first person of the parable boasts to God about his spiritual practices and condemns the other worshiper in the temple. He thinks he is a pillar of the community but actually destroys it with his judgmental attitude. He is a spiritual wreck in need of Jesus' spiritual cleansing.

The tax collector condemns no one and does not seek to impress God. He is keenly aware of the state of his heart, acknowledges his sin, and humbly asks for mercy. Humility makes our hearts the right size to enter the narrow way of Jesus.

Lord Jesus Christ, have mercy on me a sinner, and grant me your peace. Amen.

*P*aul insisted that the gospel is pure gift; we can do nothing to earn salvation. Faith, not adherence to Mosaic Law, is the one thing needed.

Some people believe in a gospel derived from fictional works, and some maintain that Jesus married, fathered a child, and died a natural death. This "different gospel" diverts attention from the living God toward speculation.

I live about two miles from "Touchdown Jesus," the huge mural on the Notre Dame library facing the football stadium. Much is made of this image during football season, but Jesus is no referee.

Some preach a prosperity Jesus; some, a hell-fire Jesus. Jesus is not a team mascot, a party-line God, or a mere mortal. Jesus refuses our labels and furnishes his: Good Shepherd, Living Bread, and Light of the World.

Let us not confuse fiction with faith or research with prayer. The gospel is simple: Jesus Christ ministered, suffered on the cross, and died, and after three days rose from death. He says, "Peace be with you, I am with you always." He is the pathway to Abba (Father), in whom we live, move, and have our being. If we abide in God, not in a novel or theories, we will have much joy.

Holy God, if we neglect you, turn us to yourself, for you are joy and light and true peace to the soul; through Christ our Lord. Amen.

Stephen worked signs and wonders among the people. One day while preaching, he looked up and saw the glory of heaven. As he described his revelation, the crowd rushed at him, throwing stones. Standing nearby was the persecutor-in-chief, who said, "I am Saul, and I approve this stoning." The next day, the entire church in Jerusalem came under siege. Saul broke into house after house, dragging out the occupants and throwing them in prison (Acts 7:54—8:3).

Saul, as Paul was formerly known, needed an intervention, and received one from God that halted him in his tracks. A short while later, he began preaching in a Damascus synagogue, stunning all who heard him.

We often find that Jesus' teaching runs counter to our natural response to people: love our enemies; withhold judgment; turn the other cheek. Our instincts are often wrong. We have much in common with the disciples who often misunderstood Jesus. To live a God-directed life, we must recognize when we are on the wrong heading, consider how our behavior and thoughts are at cross-purposes with divine love; then pray to be led the right way and to follow through.

God, help me to know myself that I may change direction as often as need be; through Christ. Amen.

*P*aul felt led to minister to Gentiles, those outside the Jewish faith. Not wishing to bring discord to the community, he met in private with the Jerusalem church leaders: James, Peter (Cephas), and John. After some discussion, they warmly approved Paul's work and set him at ease. Paul showed humility and wisdom in consulting with them. He knew those fourteen years of ministry did not exempt him from the need to seek guidance from others.

As a pastor, I realized what Paul meant when he spoke of the church as one body (1 Corinthians 12). One was the idea person; others had analytical skills; and others were great at follow-through. I was attuned to emotions, helped forestall arguments, and made sure everyone felt included. Together we functioned as one, through the varied gifts the Holy Spirit provided us.

May we live in spiritual harmony with one another that our life together may reflect the loving communion of the Holy Trinity.

God, grant me self-knowledge, that I may know when to speak, when to be silent, when to act, and when to be still, abiding in your love through Jesus Christ. Amen.

I worked the night shift at a bakery one summer packing orders of hotdog and hamburger buns. They rode a conveyor belt from oven to bagging machine night after night. The first few days, my dreams were a baker's edition of *The Sorcerer's Apprentice* with a relentless procession of buns. I am so glad that spiritual life is not like that, tedious with assigned duties and prayers as uniform as hamburger buns.

A friend told me that Christ greeted her one morning with a simple "Hi." We are not Jesus' employees charged with endless tasks; we are not his slaves, driven by fear. We are his friends.

"Christ lives in me," says Paul. We have no reason to fear union with our Savior. Paul did not become an android, robbed of personality. Christ is the vine; we remain branches, receiving life from him. We are nurtured, not obliterated.

Our faith is in our Friend who loves us. He does not clock hours, expects no adherence to mind-numbing rules, and will not chew us out if we fall short of our spiritual expectations. He only asks that we accept him and love as we are loved.

Merciful God, you are love, and I have no reason to turn away from you. Welcome me as I come home to you; through Christ my Savior. Amen.

A few days ago, my sweetheart and I returned to Lake Michigan. He tossed a bottle into the lake, and waves carried it to our feet. It contained a message that we read together: "Will you marry me?"

Both of us answering "Yes!" we hugged and laughed, then raced back to the warmth of the car. It would have been nice to be engaged in Lake Michigan, but then we would have gotten cold feet.

In marriage, husband and wife share a bond of love and trust and form a household. They become a center of stability and warmth for others.

God chooses Abraham that he may teach his children and heirs to act with compassion and justice and to trust divine love. He will radiate out blessing that will reach all nations of the earth.

God chooses you to become a center of blessing, rippling out in all directions. Will you cultivate your relationships in order to leave a legacy of faith, love, and laughter?

God, be in my heart and its loving; my mind and its knowing; my lips and their speaking; my hands in their touching; through Jesus Christ. Amen.

I lived in Mexico for several months as part of a university program. My host family had a modest home with a sunny open courtyard in the middle. Roses bloomed in huge mosaic vases. "Abuela," or "grandmother," spent hours cooking fresh yeast rolls and chicken consommé of such flavor that I would gladly have eaten them as my only food for the rest of my life. Young men strumming guitars taught us folk songs and showed us much kindness.

I cried when I returned home. When I left Mexico, I lost something very precious. I reeled at our culture's crassness and lack of warmth. Looking at American culture from the outside, I saw it to be imperfect. I had glimpsed a different way.

Our culture thrives on arrogance, callousness, gossip, aggression, violence, and self-centeredness. God's law consists of mercy, compassion, gentleness, and love. God commands us not to meddle in the affairs of others or to injure them in any way by out-of-bound emotions or behavior. God's way keeps our hearts sensitive to love and leads to joyous life.

"Do not do as everybody else does," says God; "follow my way." The world's path is deeply rutted. Love's way is a new trail blazed by the Spirit.

Loving God, transform me by the renewing of my mind and heart through Jesus Christ. Amen.

*I*n public worship, we do not curse but confess our sin. We take responsibility for our actions rather than condemn others. Sinners are not shooed away from church property but welcomed to pray with the other dense disciples, lost sheep, prodigal sons and daughters, and folks with logs sticking out of their eyes. We all seek redemption.

A couple showed up at worship one morning in my late husband's church. They took a seat in the back pew. The man's face was disfigured, and his vision was limited by an injury that had occurred years before. They dressed differently than others in the pews. One woman was offended by their presence and told them, "Your kind is not welcome here."

Several months after the couple joined the church, David asked them to distribute the bread and wine at communion. He did not curse the prejudiced church member but taught by loving, inclusive example.

May God so bless us with growing compassion and wisdom that we may recognize sin within our hearts and Christ's presence in others. With one hand, let us pull giant logs out of our eyes, and with the other, embrace our neighbors.

Gracious God, make me aware of my sins, that seeing how my actions have wounded others, I may repent of them and find forgiveness and new life in Christ my Lord. Amen.

I was standing in line at the luggage carousal after a flight. Without warning, a woman hit me in the gut with a huge, heavy suitcase she'd hoisted off the belt. I was stunned as my lungs refilled with air. The baggage thrower didn't say, "Sorry" or ask how I was.

The threat Habakkuk sees in wealth and possessions is that they can make us oblivious to others and ignorant of the state of our souls. Some people never have enough, he observes; wealth and possessions do them no good.

We already have enough stuff. We cannot buy what we lack. Jesus suggests that we travel lightly and grow rich in intangibles. By this, he does not mean trademarks or copyrights but compassion and love.

To be righteous is to trust God. We cannot purchase righteousness like a can of soup off the grocery shelf. It is given to us as we persevere through the tedium and troubles of our days. We look back and find that our prayers were answered. Each answered prayer strengthens us to lean harder on God and be bolder in prayer. "I will do whatever you ask in my name," says Jesus (John 14:13).

May we grow rich within and detached from things. May we radiate warmth and peace to everyone.

God, grant me simplicity of soul that I may love you, my neighbor, and myself; through Jesus Christ. Amen.

I have been shy and self-conscious for much of my life. Walking in front of other people in high school was excruciating, but a decade later, I was the pastor greeting others as they came to worship, offering my hand to children half-hidden behind their parents.

"We are not among those who shrink back and so are lost," says Hebrews (v. 39). This is not to say shy people are doomed. The passage discourages withdrawing from God—something hard to do since God seeks us out, hoping to establish friendship. God, endlessly patient, will pursue us and try everything to reassure us.

When we reach out with a mustard-seed-size portion of faith (trust), God rewards us with affirming love and encourages us to ask more, to be bolder, to be confident to the point of expecting everything from divine love. With God, everything is possible.

When we learn this lesson, we are no longer lost but found, no longer need be timid in prayer but confident. We are God's children; God will withhold nothing from those who take him at his word.

Resurrecting God, you know what I am capable of doing for you, and you offer me all that I need to serve you like an apostle. Help me to say, "Yes!" through Christ my Lord. Amen.

A young man asks Jesus what he needs to do to find eternal life. If giving away his lunch would make it happen, he would do it. Jesus refuses to give a quick solution. In the end, the young man leaves Jesus with pain in his heart and tears in his eyes, thinking, "I just wanted to get myself squared away with God."

Today I watched the television program that makes over cluttered homes. One of the country's messiest homes was featured. The dining table was turned on its side, and the carpet was littered with clothing. The husband's deceased grandmother, he insisted, wanted all her old furniture to stay put.

The makeover hosts worked hard to pry loose the couple's attachment to their excess goods. It is always the painful part of the show, but this time, they succeeded.

Can we allow the Holy Spirit the freedom to make us over so that detaching from all we thought was important, we may be shown what really matters? We might shed tears and find reason to complain. Don't give up and turn away when Jesus seems to ask too much. Ask for help, and you will receive the grace to take a step on his path and then another.

Gracious God, you are my treasure and my joy. Help me to love you with undivided heart; through Christ my Lord. Amen.

Y ou foolish Galatians!" fumes Paul. He has discovered that the Galatians believe faith is about what they do rather than about trusting God. Those who rely on "works," he insists, "are under a curse," ruined. Those who hear good news and believe are blessed.

When I was a student hospital chaplain, I visited an anxious man facing back surgery with an uncertain outcome. A few hours before, his wife called and announced that she was thinking of leaving him. We talked for a while and then joined hands for prayer.

As I spoke, I felt a pulsating energy that continued as long as our hands were clasped. Finally, I looked through tears of joy and said, "I feel something very powerful happening here." His face was flooded with peace. "Yes," was his simple reply. He didn't have surgery and left the hospital several days later.

That day divine love healed a man. I never learned the details: whether the cause was emotional, physical, or both. What happened was a gift of God and had little to do with me. If I had claimed credit, I would have been a fool. God saw two believers praying and blessed them.

May we trust God and pray, expecting blessing from divine love.

God, I can do nothing to earn your favor; help me accept your gracious love; through Jesus Christ. Amen.

*W*alk before me," the Lord says to Abram, "I am God Almighty." If one day while I was walking along the river, I suddenly saw God's light shimmering on the waters and had a vision of God's oceanic love, I might fall to the ground. Cars could honk, and children could point, but I wouldn't care.

We do walk before God. Divine peace shines out and flows over and within us. We could not breathe were it otherwise. We could not work or love were it otherwise. God is God to us.

In old age, God gives Abram a vision of offspring and kings, nations and land, spreading out from himself into distant time. Abram falls down to the ground. He had expected little to happen so late in life. Now God promises him everything. Joy washes over him.

"Follow me," says Jesus. Therefore, we walk. We know he is present, unfolding our path, teaching and protecting us. Christ has made us promises: of companionship, new life, an eternal home, and the possibility of bringing peace and healing to others.

May we open our hearts to embody Christ, that blessing may stream out from us like a widening river, and future generations be blessed. God is God to us!

God, unveil your presence to my soul, that finding joy in you, I may give joy to others; through Christ, my Shepherd and my Friend. Amen.

The gift of the Holy Spirit is not a strange one-time event or a seasonal occurrence but a permanent transformation that occurs over a lifetime. We begin as self-centered infants; ideally we grow into loving, gentle, and just adults, who like Mary choose to be always in Christ's presence.

If you are baptized, the promise is reality: the Holy Spirit of Christ is with you. If you give your consent to God, you will grow from selfishness into compassion; from anger into love, beauty, and glory. Day by day, it is hard to detect, but in your lifetime, you will see the grace of transformation.

The promise is also for all who are "far away," not geographically but spiritually: those without self-control; the brash, arrogant, and mean; those mired in despair; victims of the worst assaults one human can inflict on another. The Holy Spirit is intent on them; God calls them; Christ is the stranger beside them they cannot identify. How will they learn to see and hear?

Merciful God, you transform hearts and minds that we may grow to bear all the fruits of the Holy Spirit. Use me today to bring peace and strength to another; through Jesus Christ. Amen.

*W*hen I use my credit card, I earn "thank-you points." When I eat at a nearby restaurant, I get punches on a card toward a free meal. No "rewards" are free, although I am sure businesses want me to think they are gifts.

God has no incentive program; Jesus has no punch-card system. The divine is a free Spirit, operating a unique loyalty program. God reaches out first. We need not apply for acceptance and need no references. God reached out to us before we knew of God, before we were conceived, before our ancestors' births, before all time. God's compassion toward us streams out from divine infinity: we are truly blessed.

Our sins are covered; Christ has taken them into his heart and forgiven us. Had he not, we could not even stand under the spiritual weight of all we have done to offend others, our souls, and God. Christ did this without entangling us in a no-more-sinning agreement. He did it although he knew it was a sure thing we'd sin again as we stumbled after him, following the best way we know how.

God notes the bent of our hearts over time. It is not to reward us according to spiritual effort; it is *God's reminder to us* to show love as often as need be until we recognize Christ within and all our words and actions become blessing.

Blessing God, you have blessed me from the beginning of my life. Help me to live my gratitude by the grace of Christ. Amen.

Some religions have wardrobe guidelines; identifying their adherents is easy. Not so with most Christians. Our clothing is social rather than religious expression. Some schools mandate uniforms to ease tensions between those who have well-made garments and those who cannot afford them. Once students graduate, they, like all others, must learn to discern the heart and disregard outer appearance—to see as God sees.

We are all students in the school of Christ. Year after year, our task is to learn to disregard the distinctions we make between "us" and "them." It is difficult work, essential for spiritual progress. Jesus wants us to welcome sinners, hypocrites, strangers, prisoners, sick people, and children, all whom we might overlook or despise. "When you accept them, you accept me."

Look in the eyes of your neighbors and passersby, people in mug shots and those who loiter on street corners. These are your brothers and sisters, clothed with glory. Christ has wrapped them in the fabric of his being.

You also are wrapped up with Christ, one with him and all his friends. Would you remove yourself, now that you know total acceptance?

Joyous God, help me to accept myself, that I may embrace all who differ, discovering in them the presence of Christ Jesus. Amen.

*O*ne night in England, sadness weighed down my shoulders. There wasn't enough money; I washed clothes in the sink and could not find a publisher for a book on which I had labored a long time. I laid in bed unable to sleep.

In the next moment, I felt as small as a baby. Unseen parental hands surrounded me, burnishing down my rough edges. "God is at work on me," I thought, and fell asleep.

Christ is being formed in us: a passive process begun by the action of God in our baptism. We are pregnant with God. It takes nine months for a fetus to come to term. Should it be a surprise that spiritual maturity takes a lifetime? Or that the process usually leads to pain, tears, and occasional screams?

I did not meet with much disappointment when I was young. Everything I tried went well. How could I understand that my identity as a child of God does not depend on success or failure but by failing and enduring? How could I appreciate joy without having endured much sadness?

Until Christ is formed in you, have patience with yourself. You are growing from a child of God into the stature of Christ. Tears and pain will pass; joy will be forever.

God, you are shaping me until I harbor no more anger or anxiety, selfishness or stubbornness. Give me patience until Christ is formed within me. Amen.

*D*o things my way. Play by my rules. Don't feel that way. Don't talk." Some relationships are so suffocating that we scarcely know when a word, a laugh, or even a deep breath will upset another. This is stranglehold, not love.

"Stand up and walk," said Jesus to a paralyzed man (Luke 5:23). "Little girl, get up!" he charged a dead child (Mark 5:41). Christ sets people free from burdens, releases us from fear and despair. He does not ensnare or bind us; he does not entangle us in webs of expectations. He is a breath of fresh air.

Christ sets us free from our sins and mistakes. Follow me, he says. He does not care that others gossip about him or fail to understand his compassion. He encourages us to be so focused on the divine will that we too may come to be at peace in any situation.

Stand firm in the freedom God gives, and do not let others enslave you by manipulating you to put their needs before yours.

You are God's beloved, set free when Christ stretched out his arms on the cross. "Do not submit again to a yoke of slavery" (5:1).

God, have mercy on your children who are fearful and abused. Rescue them and show them your love through Christ. Amen.

*M*y mother and I were not close. She once confessed to me that she did not love me enough as an infant or hold me much. It was a revelation: who doesn't want to hold their baby?

Several years ago, the Spirit brought this verse to mind: "If my father and mother forsake me, the LORD will take me up" (Psalm 27:10). My father had abandoned me by dying. God showed me that my mother had emotionally forsaken me many years ago. I had spent years trying to convince myself otherwise, but it was better for me to accept the truth. I stopped looking to her for love she could not give. God has taken me up into a divine embrace: I am God's child.

God has loved us from the beginning, never turning away, always listening to our voices. We are members of the divine family. We reach out to Abba, our loving parent, as children who are always embraced, never spurned. We are not captives of those unable to accept us but God's children, unconditionally loved, heirs of sacred joy.

Holy Spirit, you pray in me and intercede for me with sighs too deep for words. Whenever you nudge me to pray, help me to become attentive, delighting in Christ my Lord. Amen.

*E*ven as we lash out at others in our childish sins, God
looks on us with the utmost kindness and love and offers us
an alternative. Left unchecked, infantile ways grow into major
mayhem and foolishness.

The alternative is the spiritual intervention of baptism. More
than a symbolic act, more than a charming sideshow in divine
worship, the Sacrament of Baptism incorporates us into the
mystical body of Christ and marks our rebirth as children of
the Spirit.

Though some receive a candle or towel as a remembrance,
the rebirth itself cannot be seen or touched. We do not see the
gray water of our sins blasted away by the power of the Spirit.
Yet in baptism God acts with great love and power to effect our
transformation, an event that unfolds across a lifetime.

You are a soul in process, led by the Spirit, following Christ.
The divine draws you into loving eternal arms from every path
and angle of your life. Look back to when you were foolish
or envious or when you pursued pleasures without regard for
the cost or consequences. Discern how you are different today.
Compare; contrast; thank God for the difference.

*Joyous God, continue to shape me through your Holy Spirit that
I may work for you and be gentle with all; through Jesus Christ.
Amen.*

*M*y robot does only what it was designed to do: walk a few steps, open its instrument-panel doors, and fire weapons. I found this 1950s Japanese toy at a yard sale. It has eyes but cannot see, a techno-head that cannot think. I used to think "obedience" was like this—robotlike, unthinking compliance.

Now I know that obedience can be life saving: obeying directions of an airline steward or a police, fire, or military officer, for example. Obeying Christ means, above all, listening to him. But he does not penalize us for disobedience. Following his guidance is a matter of free will.

I am a cancer survivor. In 1994, I had odd symptoms and was baffled. One night I dreamed someone left a baby in a basket at the front door. Then a voice said, "Your baby needs emergency care." The vivid dream got my attention. I phoned the doctor's office and got an appointment the same day. Had I waited, it would have been far worse for me. A follow-up dream told me that all this had occurred just in time, before the malignancy would have spread. Christ spoke to me; I listened.

Becoming obedient to Christ does not mean becoming an automaton. Christ frees; he doesn't constrain. Attend to his voice, for he brings you blessing.

Merciful God, bring your grace to those who know little joy. Free them to listen to Christ our Savior. Amen.

*W*hat are we to be? Christlike, we are to be participants in divine nature. Each day's leg of the journey is important. We cannot rest.

When I entered my mother's sick room for the last time, I was stunned: all about her was a soft shining light. After greeting her, I told her what I saw. She joked, "It's my new shampoo." What my sister and I and several others witnessed was God's love. I was so surprised that the woman who had treated me so poorly was beloved of God. I had to acknowledge that God was in her.

God has given us everything we need for life and godliness. In the glimpse of my dying mother embraced by light, God gave me a revelation to support my faith that we might persevere in goodness, knowledge, and love.

A long road stretches ahead of us. Silent surrounds us as we walk; the sun is hot and bright. It is the soul's journey. We receive few comforts but persevere anyway, being kind to all whose paths cross ours. Our home is just over the horizon, and light blazes through the doors.

Light of my heart, you give me everything I truly need so that I may learn to love without condition. Thank you for the grace of Jesus Christ. Amen.

*O*ne of my late husband's parishioners alienated people whenever she opened her mouth. She was devout and faithfully attended church, but one didn't sidle up to her at coffee hour for fear of having to duck verbal bombs.

One day her husband, a character in his own right, passed away. On the day his ashes were to be interred, I realized that I had to attend the service. I knew I could be hit by emotional fire, but I also knew that it didn't matter.

Three other people were at the cemetery: the funeral director, the pastor, and the widow. None of her children came, and no one from church showed up. I felt compassion for her and stood beside her. She inched closer as my husband began the service. I wrapped my arm around her, and she began to weep.

In Christ's presence, on sacred ground, faith led me to give love, and faith led her to receive it. The Spirit led me to lay aside my fear, and it led her to lay down her weapons. All that counts is love. Anything else can cut us off from Christ and one another.

Blessed God, help me to be a channel of your love, through the grace of Jesus Christ. Amen.

*P*aul believes that self-indulgence is an inadequate use of our freedom as children of God. Did God create us to be big spenders? Does God yearn for us to amass stunning collections of toys? God created us to love, pray, and serve; to become compassionate Christlike people.

And what was Christ like? He was unconcerned about stuff. He had no hobbies. He did not require nights out with the boys at a sports bar. He did not want designer sandals. Jesus was the least self-indulgent person who ever walked the earth. He diverted attention from himself and was extravagant in love, pouring himself out for others. He couldn't have helped us if he took frequent vacations, demanded delicacies for lunch, or spent time racing horses or camels.

Jesus beckons us, "Love one another as I have loved you" (John 15:12). He loves us without condition and with no thought of what we can do for him.

I am paring down my possessions to make room for things precious to my fiancé. When we marry, I want him to be at ease in our home. I have the freedom to keep everything, but it might send the message that I valued mementos over his company. I choose love.

God, bless those captive to fear, possessions, or troubled relationships. Bring them freedom and wisdom in Jesus Christ. Amen.

*S*everal years ago, I flew to Florida, eager to swim in the ocean again. White-capped waves lapped toward shore. Anglers held their rods and waited for tugs on the line. The waters were warm. I dove under the surface and felt cleansed.

As I write, television reporters converge on Pensacola Beach to cover the BP Gulf oil catastrophe. They lift tar balls from the sand and talk about oil slicks and birds covered in oil. We feel sick about this assault on the environment and sad for those who have lost their livelihoods.

God is joyous, loving, good, and beautiful. As we permit the Holy Spirit to transform us, we also become joyous, loving, and good and radiate spiritual beauty. Paul uses the term *flesh* to refer to human nature apart from divine influence, inclined to sin. Sin mars the divine image in us as surely as tar balls and oil deface Gulf coast beaches.

We cannot thrive when our hearts are smothered with sin. Anger, jealousy, and strife? Or joy, love, and peace? We do not want to mar the beauty God has poured into us. For the good of our souls and for the well-being of all those around us and the earth our home, we will follow the Holy Spirit.

Holy Spirit, heal everything in me that rebels against your goodness, denies your presence, and ignores your guidance; through Christ, my Lord and Savior. Amen.

 $\mathcal{M}$ ary, Mary, quite contrary, how does your garden grow?"
begins the popular English nursery rhyme. Today's text calls us
to look at how our metaphorical gardens are growing. At times,
the garden is in full bloom with the fruits of love, joy, peace,
and more that bring us a sense of accomplishment and pride.
And other moments we may be without a green thumb, with
withered, neglected, or struggling relationships that cause us to
grimace as we hear the reminder "You reap what you sow."

The author of Galatians offers practical advice for how we
might plant these gardens. We are reminded of our new identity
in Jesus Christ, an identity that is sustained by the incredible
gift of the Holy Spirit as our guide. The Spirit is our sustainer,
who yearns to tend our gardens with us, from the sowing to the
harvest, encouraging us to root all of our seeds in the hope we
find in the grace of God.

As you seek to plant and nurture in this coming season, how
will your garden grow?

*God of new creation, plant in us seeds of faith, that we may
grow into the disciples you have called us to be. Amen.*

A Colorful Garden of Possibilities

*T*he phone rings, interrupting an otherwise quiet evening at home. Who can it be? With no-call lists for telemarketers, personalized ring tones, and caller ID, much of the guesswork is now taken out of knowing who is on the other end of the line, making the unexpected phone call even more reason for excitement. But what if, rather than from a close friend or loved one, that call is from wisdom?

Proverbs personifies wisdom in the beautifully poetic language of a woman who reaches out to the world, inviting us to seek knowledge. She stands in the open, calling all who will hear to explore something beyond that which we know, which is far more valuable than anything else we could have imagined. It is a call to reorient our lives and search not for wealth and riches but for wisdom and integrity so that we may live in the paths of righteousness that are before us. It is not a call that comes lightly, as a special offer or dinner invitation, but a call to set aside the life we know and go deeper, increasing in knowledge and in faith.

Inviting God, with the call of wisdom ringing in our ears, may we have the courage to answer and risk being transformed. Amen.

The list of qualities of a good leader is a long one but usually includes wisdom. We want leaders who exercise good judgment, listen, and make educated decisions. Proverbs reminds us of the leaders who seek wisdom and in turn receive strength and prosperity. These wise leaders are ones who put their trust in God, setting aside their ambitions and seeking the wisdom that will bring justice and peace.

As you prepare to lead at home, at work, at church, and in the community, are you seeking God's wisdom? It is easy to forget to seek this wisdom and instead rely on our instincts, skills, and abilities. However, by looking to God first, we are reminded that all of these gifts for leadership come from a God who has also given us the gift of wisdom. God beckons us to seek wisdom in love so that we might be blessed and filled even as we give of ourselves.

Wisdom sustains us and replenishes us for the work we have been called to do.

God of Wisdom, help us to seek you first so that we may be filled with your wisdom. Amen.

*H*ow many mailings have you received with "preapproved" stamped in bold letters across the envelope or letter? This enticing word lures you to consider the offer with the promise that you will not be rejected. In fact, this company already knows who you are and wants you to join them even though you may not have done anything to deserve it.

So it is with God. Even before we can seek God, God reaches out to us through Jesus Christ in love. These words from Ephesians are an offer for which we have been "preapproved." And the offer is good. Through Christ, we have been freed from sin and embraced in love, brought into personal relationship with our Creator. If it sounds too good to be true based on our merits, it is. But that's the good news of God's grace. Even before the foundation of the world, we were created by a God who loved us enough to call us as God's own forever. Thanks be to God!

God, continue to reach out to us, claiming us as your own, gathering us in the grace of Christ. Amen.

*M*orning light breaks as birds chirp a melody that bounces off the glistening dew. Echoes of laughter, conversation, and tears resound between friends and strangers as relationships grow. The sun journeys from one horizon to the other, setting in a fiery sky of glowing reds and hazy purple clouds. Stars sprinkle across the darkness, brightly shining from light years away. Another day has come and gone. Did you take it all in?

In our busy lives, we often miss the moments to look at the world around us and appreciate our surroundings, from the mysterious splendor of nature to the magnificent diversity of human beings. What would happen if we took note of these moments? If we paused to watch the mother bird searching for worms or to see two friends greeting each other for a midday meal? Might we then become even more aware of God's presence in our lives? Today, take a moment, or a few moments, and look around. See the world through the eyes of the psalmist, whose lips praise God for all that is.

Lord, open our eyes, our minds, and our hearts to more fully experience the world around us, giving praise to you for all your majestic works. Amen.

*L*et me talk to the person in charge." It's a demand from those seeking answers and a response given by those who don't have them. Our lives are patterned by those who are in charge and seem to have the final say. They are the sages who remind us of what has been done in the past, the visionaries who keep us moving forward with what to do next. Many of us think we are in charge.

This passage declares that Christ is in charge. Christ the sage reminds us of our past, the firstborn of creation who dwelt among us, using examples from everyday life to teach us how we should live. And Christ is with us still, as the visionary who continues to call us into closer relationship with God, offering the promise of eternal life through his death and resurrection.

Talking to the one in charge is a good approach to daily living. In this, we are challenged to put Christ first so that all we say and all we do might be reflections of our faith in him.

Jesus, help us to put you first so that we may glimpse what it is like to dwell in the fullness of God. Amen.

*W*e spend an incredibly high percentage of our time waiting. As we wait, we are hopeful for good things, like a child who eagerly looks to wrapped presents under a tree. We wait in line at the grocery store or bank, for phone calls and e-mails to be returned, for the birth of a child or grandchild, for tough times to end, for test results to be revealed, and more. Waiting is an inevitable part of life, and it isn't always easy.

Even the early Christians, with the good news of Christ's resurrection ringing in their ears, waited. In the midst of challenging times, waiting kept them strong as they turned to their faith as a foundation. Like the early Christians, we are united in faith by Christ's promise of God's glory. And, like the early Christians, we must cling to the hope of that promise unseen. As we wait, may we be inspired to have the hope we read about in Romans, guided by faith and sustained by patience, trusting in a God who has gone before us.

Eternal God, we live in a world of waiting that often longs for instant gratification. Grant us the patience and the faith to place our hope in you. Amen.

*W*hat is life-giving for you? When are those moments where your energies are renewed? Perhaps these times are marked by quiet and reflection, with a morning cup of coffee by a sunny window, spending time in thought and prayer. Perhaps these times are marked by sound and engagement, reconnecting in meaningful conversation with friends and family, encouraging one another through good times and bad. We seek these moments as times when we can center ourselves once again so that we may be replenished for the work we have to do.

Proverbs 8:35 suggests that wisdom is life-giving and brings favor with the Lord. Naturally, we want to seek this wisdom, but where is it? Earlier verses paint a fantastic image of creation, locating wisdom in depths and mountaintops alike, hardly a specific location. Maybe such ambiguity brings with it hope, with the notion that God's wisdom is not limited to a particular time and space. It is free to be a part of all creation, meeting us in the starry skies and the stormy seas. May we notice the wisdom woven into our lives and find life-giving moments free from limitations of time and space.

Live-giving God, help us to seek your wisdom, that we may be renewed today. Amen.

The beginning of March is hardly what we think of as a new year. Yet today's passage reflects God's instruction to Moses and Aaron to make Abib, likely in March or April, the first month in Israel's priestly ritual calendar. The date connects to the month of the exodus, reminding Israel of its deliverance from Egypt (see Exodus 13:4). With this date God provides a list of instructions for how to begin the celebration of Passover. As the Israelites celebrate their liberation, they mark the occasion with rituals that remind them of their history as a people. These rituals are worship completed in honor of the God of salvation.

We still have many rituals that mark our time, whether at the beginning of the day, week, month, or year. We pay bills, complete chores, go grocery shopping, and more. Consider your rituals and routines. Which of these remind you of your faith? Which encourage you to reflect on God's presence in your life? What times in your pattern of living have you set apart for worship?

Lord, each day you give us the opportunity for new beginnings. As we start anew each day, bind us closer to you in worship. Amen.

*I*magine the last time your jaw dropped in amazement: at an incredible sunset, an unbelievable demonstrated skill, a decadent dessert. In our moments of awe, we can become transfixed, overwhelmed by what is before us, barely even able to utter, "Wow." Such moments are humbling, as we experience something that is out of the ordinary. Such moments are also intriguing, as we long to decipher how or why a particular event takes place.

The psalmist looks around at all of the incredible ways God has shown love for creation and responds in praise. "Holy and awesome" are the words that come to mind. This awe is just the beginning. It evokes a fear that reminds us that our God is a powerful God, capable of extraordinary things. Although we might be tempted to shy away from this fear, we are challenged to embrace it with reverence. For here we find the beginning of wisdom and can begin to delight ourselves in the many incredible things God has done.

God, your wondrous deeds surround us, and we are left in awe. Enter into our amazement and fear, that we may grow in your wisdom and forever praise your name. Amen.

*C*hances are you've read this passage before, probably a few times. It's tempting to skim through these first verses in the Bible, eager to get to the creation of plants, animals, and humans. But go back and read these first words again, slowly.

Before all that was, God was there. A wind from God, perhaps likened to a deep breath or mighty wind, stirs the waters. Chaos ensues. Out of chaos, God says, "Lighten up." This light doesn't still the chaos. It illuminates the world in the day, exposing the fury of creativity that will follow in the next five days. So it is with our lives. God comes in as a mighty wind, enlivening us by the Spirit, turning our world upside down, and creating something new. In the midst of newness, light shines.

As your world is turned upside down with newness, where are you in the chaos? Are you swirling among the waters? Blinded by the light of day? Groping through the darkness of night? Can you go back to the beginning, to the source of all that is, and dwell in God's Spirit?

Almighty God, enliven us with your Spirit, and illumine us with your light, even in the midst of chaos. Amen.

*N*ews travels quickly. Late-breaking news interrupts our regularly scheduled programming to make sure we are aware of the latest important happenings in the world. Phones ring and e-mail inboxes fill with good news of engagements and births. Each day, we hear more and more information that keeps us "in the loop."

When we encounter someone who isn't as well versed as we are, we might be caught by surprise. "How could you possibly not have heard about that?" we wonder. The prophet Isaiah voices a similar refrain. Following the joyful promise of a new age in which the glory of the Lord will be revealed, Isaiah marvels in God's creative works. Then, as if someone has said, "Wait; who is this God?" Isaiah offers a quick rhetorical summary, bringing things back to the very foundations, rooting God's promise in the very beginning of time.

When we share our faith with others, it is easy to take much for granted in our listeners. But perhaps we do well to follow Isaiah's example and recap the foundations of our faith, grounding our journey in praise.

We have heard, Lord, but need to hear it again. Strengthen our foundations, and lead us into greater understanding of you. Amen.

*M*ovie trailers are highly evolved art forms. They pique our interest with funny one-liners, the beginning of a pivotal moment, or a cliffhanger that leaves us begging for more. If they've done their job, trailers persuade us to return to the theater to view the movie.

John gives the people a preview of what is to come. He presents a famous quote from Isaiah, referencing the rich history of the people of Israel, who still remind one another of how they were called out of the wilderness into the promised land. There's an action sequence, as John baptizes in the Jordan, offering cleansing from sin. And there's the teaser of a pivotal moment, with the promise of one who is even more powerful who will come with the Holy Spirit.

Immediately, we recognize that the one to come is Jesus, the same one who will later leave the tomb empty. It is like a movie based on a well-loved book or a favorite film we return to repeatedly. Knowing the story so well, can we get excited about it again? Can we continue to be transformed by this good news?

Creative God, continue to spark our imaginations, so we may long to hear your story. Amen.

*H*ow many times have you read Scripture and felt baffled by its meaning? As you try to wrap your head around certain passages, you might wonder why they are included in the Bible. At the very least, you have a handful of questions about how it all fits together.

As the risen Christ prepares to say goodbye, he calls the disciples to remember all that he has told them, combined with the Scripture they already know. He reminds them that his presence bears witness to these texts. But he also recognizes that they are going to need some help figuring out what it all means. His final words are a promise: the Spirit of God will return to them, guiding them into what is to come.

Like the disciples, we can rest in the promise that we are not alone in our study of Scripture. We have been given the gift of community, gathering places in which to read and study together. And we have been given the gift of the Holy Spirit, who continues to inspire our reading of God's word. We are not alone, thanks be to God!

Lord, send your Spirit among us. Amen.

The Gospel of John begins with those beautiful abstractions, so mysterious, so puzzling: "In the beginning was the Word and the Word was with God. . . ." Yet within that mystery is the most profound truth of Christianity—God moved in and pitched a tent among us; moved in and became one of us, a brother, a neighbor; moved in and set up shop to build the kingdom. Despite the bad neighborhood, the cruelty, death, and disease that inhabit the place, God moves in. Despite darkness and a poor welcome, God moves in. Despite hopelessness and despair, God moves in. And suddenly, the place looks better. The darkest places are set about by light. Now there is hope.

All of us have found ourselves walking in shadow, living with hopelessness, surrounded by darkness. Where do you find the darkness in which you must walk? How has the light of God's love and compassion moved in for you? Where have you found the pitched tent of God's understanding and wisdom and been able to see the places of light? Look next door. The kingdom of God is that close.

Lord, help us walk in your light. Amen.

I 've done what you asked. I've finished this task": Jesus says that God has given him glory and authority to bring the world to God. And he prays, in this last prayer before his death, that he has accomplished the work that shows God's majesty and beauty. God is given glory—the world is lit up brilliantly with the love of the Son and the Father. Yet at the last, Jesus prays once again to be in the presence of God's glory as he was before the beginning of all things.

What is he asking? He asks to give up the flesh that made him one of us. But for John, the incarnation is what it was all about. Jesus had restored the connection between Creator and creation. Jesus brings us all before the throne of grace. No matter what he must face now, Jesus has restored that union. He prays with confidence to the Father who sent him. And he points us toward a truth: in whatever we face, God is with us.

We give glory to you, O God, knowing that Jesus came to bind us all in community. Amen.

"You search the Scriptures. . . ." People have always scoured Scriptures to find their ideas affirmed there. Someone once said that too many people use Scripture as a drunk uses a lamppost—more for support than illumination. A little harsh, perhaps, but we are all guilty of doing exactly that. We want to take the parts we like and pretend the rest is irrelevant or misunderstood, containing meaning that some are too dense to grasp. In this passage, we are reminded that this approach to Scripture is a perpetual failing. Jesus reminds us that Scripture points us to God; Scripture, he asserts, points to Jesus. When we try to bend Scripture's meaning to our will, we miss the revelation. We miss the good news. We miss the blinding light of God's glory because we have shuttered ourselves inside our opinions.

We are reminded in these verses to pay attention to the proclamation throughout Scripture and, as the writer of 1 Peter 3:15 tells us, to "be ready to make your defense to anyone who demands from you an accounting for the hope that is in you."

Open our eyes, Lord, to your glory. Amen.

*W*hat credentials do you have to speak the way you do? Jesus teaches with power. He has already irritated the temple authorities, yet he teaches. And he does so without special training, without degrees or plaudits or published works or recommendations from established experts. Now, this is no argument for untrained preachers, but it does remind us that we are talking about listening for a word from God and not to the credentials of the speaker.

Perhaps it is a reminder to stop, put away our distractions, our worries, our cell phones, and listen hard. We may find ourselves in disagreement. Perhaps we become uncomfortable. In this chapter of John, though, Jesus reminds his listeners that he speaks to give honor and glory to the One who sent him. He is not offering rules that must be followed for God to be honored. He is offering the chance for us to put aside our preconceptions and to follow God's voice at Jesus' transfiguration: "This is my Son . . . listen to him."

Gracious God, open our ears, our hearts, our minds when we are reluctant to listen. Amen.

There are harsh words in this chapter between Jesus and his opponent. For the Johannine community, they reflected the disputes between Judaism and the Christian sect that challenged the role of the law. These disputes echo in today's political climate—one side demonizing the other: "Liar." "Demon." "Who do you think you are?" "What else can you expect from an outsider?" "You know they don't worship the way we do."

It is easy—and dangerous—to read these passages and find justification for the most extreme kind of sectarianism. The language of hate obscures the real question. Is excluding others the only way to establish our identity? Is to say who we are not the only way to establish who we are? Perhaps, sometimes, for an oppressed community of faith, it is an option.

But for us, it must not be. Jesus claims the name of God—"I am," he says. "I was even before Abraham." These are the words drawing us into God's presence, affirming that Jesus Christ is Lord. We stand on this rock. In confidence, we can reach beyond barriers that divide us.

Lord, help us reach out in love. Amen.

There is a saying you sometimes hear in church discussions about worship: "It's not about you; it's about God." There's bold truth in that. Despite all that Jesus had done, there were those who would not believe, who continued to think he was merely a distraction, who found his presence threatening to the status quo.

And those who did believe? Well, they kept their mouths shut. They could not risk their positions, their reputations, their glory.

Does faith finally come down to giving ourselves away, of showing to the world a generous heart and giving up our desire for worldly praise? These are not easy things to do, but how else do we shift the focus of the church away from vending spiritual services to those demanding it and move toward true discipleship? The prophet Jeremiah reminds us that when we find ourselves afraid to claim God, God will always keep covenant with us: "I will put my law within them, and I will write it on their hearts; and I will be their God, and they shall be my people" (31:33b).

Lord, be a light for us, a guide for us, on the path where you lead. Amen.

$\mathcal{J}$esus brings us together. To God, he prays that all may be brought together as God intended from the beginning of time. But we have to listen hard to these verses—Jesus says he has made known to the disciples the love of God. Do they come together with that knowledge? Do worldly fears hold them back? Unity is a goal, but lack of trust divides.

It is the great strength of evil to pull people apart, to make us believe we are separate and unequal. But this is not what we are meant for. We are unique; we have our gifts to offer in relationship. But more to the point, we cannot be Christians by ourselves. We cannot do spiritual life as a solo. We are meant to be together, united in Christ. We partake in the reconciliation that Jesus proclaims. Imagine what our lives might be like when God answers the prayer Jesus offers.

To be one in God, made so by the glory of Jesus Christ—this is joy. This is life. For this, we give thanks. To God be the glory.

Lord, join us together; connect us to one another by your love. Amen.

*W*e remember our moms asking us to do things around the house: "Set the table"; "Feed the dog"; "Empty the trash." We usually had no choice about doing what was expected of us. It was the way we learned to be responsible members of our family.

At a wedding in Cana—likely that of an extended family member—Jesus' mom asks him to help keep the party going by providing some wine. He's not ready to reveal himself as God's Son, so he tries to keep from doing what she requests. But moms being moms, Jesus eventually does what she expects—and does it exceptionally well! Only the servants and his mom know where the wine comes from—his concession to remaining anonymous while being a responsible member of the family.

As members of the family of God, we too are asked to help: pray for a friend; feed a family; financially support the church's work; serve on the session; volunteer in the nursery. Do we respond joyously or with hesitation?

God of our life, help us answer with joy and give our best effort when you call us to serve our family. Amen.

*W*e've all been afraid of the dark. We've longed for the gloom to be transformed by a welcome light—the sun, the moon, a campfire, a flashlight, an electric lamp, even a tiny appliance LED.

In a most remarkable sermon, Jesus tells us to become "the light of the world" (v. 14) and to "let our light shine before others" (v. 16). He seems certain we can help others in the dark places of their existence. How do we bring the reassurance of a welcome "light" into dark places . . . especially when we feel we have nothing to offer?

Even the darkest place on earth has a minuscule bit of light. Every person has something to share with another: a smile, a hug, a kind word, a book, a conversation, a casserole, a ride to the grocery story, an offer to babysit, an invitation to lunch or to church. Jesus asks that we share a little of ourselves—to bring what light we can to a dark and hurting world.

Holy One, may we find a bit of light to share with others, that our lives may be warmed by your comforting presence. Amen.

The *Twilight* saga by Stephanie Meyer has captured the minds of many young people, especially those desiring the intense romance portrayed in the novels. Some even create "families" with others who are also enchanted by the shadow world of vampire and werewolf legends. They believe themselves to be friends with the terrors of deep darkness; some rebel against the light of their Christian heritage to the point of declaring themselves agnostics.

The primary developmental task of young people is to question and rebel against what adults have taught them—a search for self that confuses many of the trusted adults in their lives. A seemingly normal young person becomes someone completely unrecognizable . . . except to those who know this as a normal part of young adulthood. The secret is to allow young people enough space to explore various ideas so they can truly claim what is genuine and authentic for them.

God allows that, too—it's called free will. God gives us enough space to question, rebel, and then decide who we are and whose we are.

Loving God, stay with us when we are searching so we can find our way back to you when we are done. Amen.

*I*magine a poster of a kitten struggling to hang on to a rope. The caption reads something like "When you come to the end of your rope, tie a knot and hang on." For people in the midst of such a precarious situation, the poster could cause them to scream, "I don't know how to tie a knot!"

When my younger brother was dying, I desperately needed something to hang onto. I told God that Mike should be doing something other than lying in a hospital bed, suffering the devastating effects of myelofibrosis. I wanted my athletic, good-looking, wisecracking brother to be running a marathon or coaching his daughters in soccer; he was too young to be preparing to join our parents in eternal life. God's comforting love gave me something to hang on to, something to share with family and friends . . . and with Mike.

For me, God's love is like a knot at the end of a rope that doesn't need tying because it's just there . . . ready to hold when the rope starts swaying.

Eternal God, thank you for sending your steadfast love to surround us when we need it the most—and especially when we don't even know we need it. Amen.

There are visual learners who can easily retrieve information that they have seen. Then there are auditory learners who remember better when they hear things. Still others are kinesthetic learners for whom the experience of physically doing something allows them to retain knowledge better. There are many ways to learn; one method is no better than another.

God wants us to seek forgiveness when we've done something inappropriate. Asking pardon from God or a human being offers us an opportunity to grow emotionally and spiritually. Like the Israelites, we can use reminders—spiritual disciplines—to help us grow and live into the persons God created us to be. Perhaps it's an inspirational painting, poster, or ceramic figurine; it might be a chant, hymn, or classical work; or it could be a particular pose, a set of movements, or a dance. Whatever it is speaks to us of God's love and our inability to live complete lives without God's help.

God of all life, we often turn away from the path you've chosen for us. May the reminders we use keep our faces turned toward you. Amen.

$\mathcal{M}$y friend, the wife of a career army officer, has an only son named Jason. The year he turned fourteen, she was in much turmoil about the length and style of his hair. Her husband was also very concerned that Jason keep his hair groomed in a military fashion. They both devoted much time, anguish, and prayer to the matter—not to mention having many unpleasant conversations with Jason.

Finally, the distress ended; I desperately wanted to know how harmony had been restored to the family. My friend told me that she and her husband had spent some time considering Jason's character and behavior. They had reached the conclusion that if he was not breaking any of the Ten Commandments, not putting himself or others in danger, and was keeping up his grades and church attendance, they would no longer worry about such things as his hair. They realized that Jason was a wonderful young man and a godly person (who is now an elder), and that their son's haircut did not reflect badly on them.

O God, may we follow you all of our lives and live by your commandments, sacrificing our human standards when they interfere with yours. Amen.

We need to be reminded of God's activity in our lives. It may take years before we're able to look back and see God's handiwork; if we're lucky it doesn't take that long.

Youth and adults from several congregations came together for a week-long Habitat for Humanity work camp in West Virginia. The week before we left, I was juggling leadership responsibilities for the work camp and the congregation's participants along with the usual congregational tasks. The church office had just relocated to temporary quarters, and our phone provider was not in any hurry to provide coverage. My professional colleague in ministry was away, and my iPhone was constantly busy with texts, phone calls, and e-mails.

I knew what to expect during the work camp: dirty bodies, dirty clothes, sore muscles, short tepid showers, shared sleeping quarters, on-the-spot decision making—and no cell coverage. I hadn't been without cell coverage in years! God knew I needed to recharge my personal batteries by serving just where I was. It was physically demanding but spiritually nourishing and refreshing! Try it sometime.

Almighty God, you humble us when you provide exactly what we need; help us to appreciate how well you care for us. Amen.

*W*hile the older children in vacation Bible school were preparing PowerPoint presentations to illustrate the creation narrative, we naturally fell into discussions of science versus Scripture. Where was God before the world began? How did God create light? What does the Milky Way really look like? Is Earth the only place in the universe that has life? Such good questions—and the children provided such good answers:

God just was; God made the Big Bang happen so light could be created; we can't see all the stars in our galaxy while we're inside it; God isn't selfish and so did not create life only on the Earth.

Later in the week, we tackled the Emmaus story of the two disciples who were joined by Christ but didn't recognize him until he blessed and broke bread with them. They had a comment on that one too: God helps us understand about Jesus when it's time for us to understand . . . but it's not an explanation—you just know.

Loving God, you sent your Son that we might live with you eternally. For your amazing gift and our childlike faith that just knows, we thank you. Amen.

September 11, 2001, was a day of complexity in the Washington, D.C., area. I watched the horrific events occurring on my television screen while on the phone checking on family, friends, and congregants at the Pentagon or in New York City. We didn't know then, but we were to experience the miracle of parishioners walking out of the Twin Towers and the Pentagon . . . and the tragedy of losing many in our community.

That night, the local faith communities came together in our sanctuary—Jews, Catholics, Protestants, Muslims, Sikhs, Unitarians, and even some who claimed no faith. Some felt that God had abandoned us that day; others had cause to celebrate that their loved ones were safe. We sang and prayed together and sincerely listened to one another. Those of us who led the service felt that God was indeed present with us, even though deceitful and unjust individuals were the cause of our deep anger and sadness. By the end of the service, we were united in our hope in God—an awesome miracle on such a tragic day!

Everlasting God, deliver us from the deceitful and unjust people in this world. Continue to "send out your light and your truth" that we may always be comforted. Amen.

*W*hile discussing baptism with a confirmation class, a young lady told us she had baptized her guinea pig and wondered if that act made her guinea pig a Christian. As we discussed that question and the meaning of baptism, we came to the conclusion that just going through the motions did not make a person—or a guinea pig—a Christian. There has to be some knowledge of God and a belief in Jesus Christ as Lord and Savior in order to request the Sacrament of Baptism. It required knowledge on the part of the individual or his or her parents.

Knowledge comes in many forms: formal classroom education, prayer, conversation, participation in a mission project—they all teach us something if we are open to receiving the lesson. As a Christian educator, I take very seriously and literally Christ's commission to "go . . . and make disciples, baptizing them . . . and teaching them . . . " (Matthew 28:18–20). This commission is not exclusive to educators; all Christians carry the responsibility. How are you living out Christ's commission?

Teach me your way, O Lord, that I may walk in your truth, and I will glorify your name forever. Amen.

*I*t wasn't your average evening in the garden in the Kidron valley when Jesus went to pray. John painted a clear word picture of his version of the events. Judas brought a detachment of soldiers and some police to arrest his friend Jesus. Peter got sword happy defending Jesus and cut off another man's ear. Jesus was the only one in control, knowing exactly what would happen, and twice volunteered his name to the arresting forces.

Because of its significance, all four of the Gospel writers recorded the event. Each one told the story, with slight variations, but the basics remained the same. This set of events marked the beginning of the end for Jesus. He knew he would die, yet he graciously cooperated with his captors so his friends would not be harmed.

Few people ever have to make a decision to save others' lives knowingly by giving theirs. Such selfless love is an amazing gift to those for whom it is offered. Jesus gave himself for his friends and all of humanity. That knowledge humbles me beyond all words.

Eternal One, your love for us is overwhelming! We are speechless when we remember your unfathomable gift, and we thank you with all our being. Amen.

$\mathcal{J}$esus had been arrested; some of his disciples followed him into the high priest's courtyard. Peter stayed outside—perhaps scared and unable to truly believe what had just happened. Another disciple called for Peter to come inside, but a woman questioned him, "You are not also one of this man's disciples, are you?" (v. 17). Uncertain how to behave, Peter denied being one of Jesus' disciples and tried to blend into the crowd, standing near a fire to warm himself.

It was a very human thing to do—protecting himself at all costs. But this was Peter—the foundation of Jesus' church! Why was he lying; why was he not declaring himself as one of Jesus' disciples? Didn't he just cut off a man's ear to protect Jesus from being arrested? How could Jesus possibly name him as the one to lead the church?

Fear changes people. Some freeze and can't even speak; others seemingly become another person—sometimes babbling or unable to control their bodies. It's the exceptional person who can face his or her fears and move beyond them. How do you face your fears?

Sheltering God, when we are afraid, guide us back to your comforting love. Amen.

*I*n contrast to a cowering Peter, Jesus remained calm during questioning. He defined himself through the words and actions he had taken during his ministry: "I have said nothing in secret" (v. 20). The police didn't know how to respond to him and sent him along to the high priest Caiaphas. He may have been God's Son, but he was also a human being and experienced events as a human. He must have been at least a bit concerned.

My lawyer friends suggest that defending yourself in open court is not a good concept. They suggest retaining a counselor who can research the laws, ask insightful questions, and deliver appropriate words without the emotion the defendant might bring to the experience. Jesus had the best Counselor available for his defense—the Holy Spirit. The research was in hand, the right questions were offered, and the correct words spoken on his behalf. The Spirit was there during the questioning, and the Creator remained at his side through all the horror that was to come.

Holy Comforter, we need you in our lives when people question our actions, our words, our motives. Guide our responses that we might glorify God in all that we do. Amen.

*T*he meeting to finalize the construction budget for the new sanctuary was under way. The visiting church matriarchs and patriarchs were there to ensure the new space would inspire those who entered through its magnificent appointments. The architect presented her list of preferred materials—all beautiful, all luxurious—almost within budget. Many elders wanted the space to be greener and less expensive. Energy costs were escalating, and they wanted to find alternatives to the stained-glass walls surrounding the chancel. They favored materials that were more in keeping with their commitment to be good stewards of the earth.

It was obvious that resolving a final construction budget would take more time. There were many considerations to be examined, and several elders requested experts in various disciplines to speak to those issues. The leaders would make the decision, but there would be pressure from various interest groups. It would be difficult to discern the truth of the situation; much prayer would be required.

God of all life, when we are faced with making important decisions, give us listening ears to hear all concerns and discerning minds to recognize the truth of the matter. Amen.

---

*W*hat does it mean if Jesus is King of the Jews? For the high priests, it's all about power and control—or the fear of losing it. Jesus is a threat to their way of life, so they use the laws to maintain status quo. It's easier than trusting God.

Control is always an illusion. In the face of a crisis, we believe that if we have a plan, we can control things and change the outcome. Or so we think. The irony is that we miss the bigger picture, just like the priests. Did you notice that when the Jewish police take Jesus to Pilate, they refuse to go inside for fear of defiling themselves for the Passover, the celebration to commemorate God's freeing the Israelites from slavery? They cannot see that God is the one in charge. They cannot fathom the freedom Jesus is offering because they are afraid of change.

When we are mired in our plans and solutions, we miss the peace and freedom that comes with trusting God. What are you trying to control in your life that you won't trust to God? Why? What are you afraid of?

Gracious God, free us from our need to control things. Amen.

God's grace is truly extravagant! How else to describe how God continues to forgive and love us despite our sin? We're not unusual. It's important to remember there are a lot of folks in the Bible whom God uses for divine purpose—people like David, Paul, and Timothy, to name a few—despite the fact they all made some mighty poor decisions.

With God, nothing is wasted. Some of our greatest learning and our best opportunities for deepening and sharing our faith arise out of our worst transgressions. We understand this on an intellectual level but not always in our hearts. God's mercy is a given. The hard part is acceptance. We aren't so good at forgiving ourselves and accepting God's grace when we have sinned. We continue to beat ourselves up long after God has forgiven us.

Do you truly repent when you offer a prayer of confession? Do you truly hear the good news of the gospel that you are forgiven? Do you allow grace to change your life?

Merciful God, thank you for the grace that overflows with the faith and love that are in Christ Jesus. Amen.

This type of mob scene is not unfamiliar to us. We hear about angry mobs and protests in the news on a regular basis. People are passionate about whatever cause or issue they support or oppose. Some fully understand the issue, and some act largely on passion. Some are so extreme as to call for violence. The mob pronounces judgment and seeks action. With few changes, this account in John could have been in today's paper.

Try to place yourself in the scene. Where do you find yourself? Are you carried away by the passion of the moment, shouting, "Crucify him!"? Are you one of Jesus' followers on the edge, stunned to silence? Are you trying to incite counter protestors or merely observing?

We have a certain responsibility to seek justice on behalf of the oppressed—to think rationally and not through the will of an angry crowd.

God, give us the courage to speak out against injustice. Amen.

*O*ne of the jobs of a parent is to teach boundaries, sometimes repeatedly. It's how kids learn right and wrong even though it doesn't always make sense at the time. God does the same with us. Much of Leviticus seems arcane: a bunch of detailed laws that appear to have no connection to our lives today. Yet the law is a part of Holy Scripture and is authoritative for us.

Understanding the law from a larger perspective is one thing that binds us together as the people of God. The law changes and evolves throughout the Torah because time and social conditions change, as they do today. But the basic laws of society—the Ten Commandments, how we treat others, and social justice—form us as a community. Jesus made it pretty simple, distilling all the laws into the Great Commandment: Love the Lord our God with all your hearts, mind, and strength, and your neighbor as yourself. Sounds easy, doesn't it?

Thank you, God, for providing us with boundaries and guiding us back when we stray. Amen.

*P*ick your worst day, multiply by a lot, and maybe you'd have a sense of what it was like to be present at the crucifixion. Maybe. This was not how things were supposed to go. Jesus of Nazareth sure seemed to be the Messiah. But now there he is hanging on a cross. A dead messiah isn't really much of messiah, is he? What are you supposed to believe now?

The incontrovertible truth is on the cross right before your eyes. Jesus told you this would happen, that he would be leaving, *and* that he would return. But did you really believe this is what he meant? You left your home, gave up everything to follow him. You were full of hope; you anticipated great change. Now what?

No, I don't think you can ever know the total sense of loss that day. Can you imagine a life without Jesus in it?

O God, where are you? Why have you forsaken us? We long to praise your name. Amen.

Trust is hard. If we're honest, don't we think those people who trust easily are a little naïve? Maybe we're just jealous. Most of us have been hurt by someone we trusted at some point in our lives. But if we are unable to have trust in God, whom can we trust? Jesus trusted God enough to give his very life—in an excruciating manner. Not only was he obedient; his last words were to commend himself into God's hands. That's some kind of trust. We know the outcome; that alone should be sufficient basis for trust.

There's much to be learned from the Psalms about trusting God. The psalmist writes from a place of relationship with and deep trust in God. He trusts enough to rage about the injustice or the pain being suffered. It's okay to be mad; God can take it and will not disappear. It's like when we say, "I love you, but I am really angry with you right now." Jesus certainly seems to have taken comfort from the Psalms.

Ineffable God, we thank you for your abiding presence in our lives. Help us to trust you even in our darkest hours. Amen.

*R*itual is important. In the midst of grief, there is great comfort in doing what is familiar, in carrying out our funeral rituals and liturgy. As Christians, reading the familiar Scriptures, singing beloved hymns, celebrating a loved one's life, remembering, and commending that beloved one to God are just what we do. It doesn't make the grief disappear, but it's a step on the journey. We find solace and hope in the promise of the resurrection.

What a beautiful story. Joseph, a secret disciple, seeks permission from Pilate to take Jesus' body. He then performs the rituals for a Jewish burial with Nicodemus, because that was how they cared for the dead. It was important to honor Jesus in this way and likely provided some comfort to Jesus' followers who were not only grieving Jesus' death but were also bereft. They had given up everything to follow their teacher, their Messiah, and now—they had nothing. What should they believe? What should they do? For the moment, the rituals were enough.

What rituals will you perform today as you grieve Jesus' death?

God of life, we, too, wait patiently, living in the hope and promise of Jesus' resurrection. Amen.

It is a dark and sad morning when Mary Magdalene visits Jesus' tomb and makes the discovery that his body is no longer there. In shock, she runs back to tell Peter and the other disciples. They go and see that Jesus is not where he had been laid to rest. Later Jesus appears to the disciples in the room where they have been hiding. He brings them words of peace and reassurance of his resurrection.

Preachers often highlight that a woman was the first to discover Jesus' resurrection and the first to proclaim the good news to others. Easter sermons hail Mary Magdalene as the first evangelist, but is this really the main focus of today's text? We are all (male and female) called to tell the good news of Christ's victory over death. Just as Christ brought peace to the hurting and frightened disciples, we can be agents of peace to a hurting and frightened world today.

Lord, in the dark places and times of this life, may we have the courage of Mary Magdalene and all the disciples to be witnesses to your life and resurrection. Infuse in us the will to act as agents of peace to all. Amen.

King David had planned to build a permanent home for the Ark of the Covenant, but God's plan was different. It must have been hard for David to swallow his pride and acknowledge that God had nixed his plans, choosing instead David's son, Solomon, to build the temple.

As a parent of two grown children, I find it difficult sometimes to release my ideas and say to my adult child, "You take over and do it your way. You will do better than I would."

King David accepted God's will and passed the planning torch to Solomon. David's final words to Solomon, in verses 9 and 10, can serve as an inspiration:

And you, my son Solomon, know the God of your father, and serve him with single mind and willing heart; for the LORD searches every mind, and understands every plan and thought . . . Take heed now, for the LORD has chosen you to build a house as the sanctuary; be strong, and act.

Sovereign God, you are in charge; we are not. Help us to remember that fact. May we strive to serve you with a single mind and a willing heart. Grant us the courage to be strong and act. Amen.

The psalmist has great plans—build a home for God, a place of rest for the mighty Ark of the Covenant. In an affirmation of these grand plans, God chose Zion to be God's forever home.

David vowed to God that he would not rest until God could reside in the place that David would find for God. God affirms David's devotion by asserting that God has chosen Zion for God's holy habitat.

In this psalm, we read of God's promise to David. God promises to set one of David's sons on the throne. God will not back down—God's promises to us are sure. Zion has been chosen, and we are the inheritors of that election.

Remember how grand it felt to be chosen to be on the kickball team? Multiply that by a million times and that is how marvelous it is to know that God has chosen you and promises to be with you forever.

Ever-faithful God, your promises to David were true, and through Jesus Christ they are true for us today. We pray that we are worthy to be your dwelling place and that we may abide with you forever. Amen.

*I*srael had forgotten the sacred rituals. They had not kept the Passover as God had commanded. They had lost touch with the elements of their faith that served as critical touchstones and reminders of their identity as children of God.

Life can get out of control. The rituals of faith that keep us connected, that satisfy our longing to be with God, can easily be pushed aside. Our spiritual identity can become lost in day-to-day activities. The daily grind can grind the faithfulness right out of our lives.

The Israelites needed to be reminded of the importance of making time to properly worship God. We, too, may need that extra push to get up and get to church when the temptation would be to do anything else. Like the Israelites of King Hezekiah's time, we require help to find our way back to regular worship and the spiritual practices of our faith that teach, inspire, and feed us.

O Lord, forgive my complacency. Fill me with a desire for you that is so strong I can do nothing less than to put aside all earthly concerns and run to meet you. I pray never to forget who I am and whose I am. Amen.

I was glad when they said to me, 'Let us go to the house of the LORD!' " (v. 1). If you are of a certain age, when you hear those words, you instantly hear in your head the song you learned in Sunday school as a child.

This psalm was a song of pilgrimage, a psalm sung as one entered the place of worship after a long journey, fulfilling an intense longing to be in the most holy of places.

What if someone who was not taken to church as a child or who has not lived life regularly attending worship reads these words? What then? How does this psalm resonate for that person?

Whether one is always in worship or rarely attends worship, verses 6–9 of this simple psalm are a powerful prayer. The prayer for peace within the walls of our homes, in our places of work and worship, for our family and friends, and for the world is something we can all embrace.

Sovereign God, we know that when justice and peace fail in your kingdom, then all are in peril. Grant us peace, but, more important, make us hungry to worship you, to engage in justice and hospitality so that we may help seekers find their way to you. Amen.

The story of young Jesus' getting separated from his parents and being found several days later at the temple in Jerusalem touches anyone who is a parent. Even if you are not a parent, parts of this story speak to the child within each of us.

Losing a child in a crowd is horrifying, but that may not be the main message in this text. Jesus' reminder to his parents that he has another parent besides the two of them is a key point to take away from this passage. How painful it must have been for Mary and Joseph to hear the words "I must be in my Father's house." The text even tells us that they did not understand him.

Reexamine this text, and find comfort in the knowledge that we have a heavenly parent—God. A friend once said to me that when her elderly parents died she felt she was an orphan. I wonder if this text is in some sense reassuring us that we are never orphans because in God we have a loving parent, a parent in whose presence we, like Jesus, may grow in wisdom and favor.

Loving, Protector God, remind us that we can never be orphaned and that we always have a home in your arms. Amen.

The words *zeal, zealous,* or *zealots* may not have positive connotations in our culture. Being zealous often alienates one from "middle-of-the-road" friends or family. The psalmist's zeal for God's house has consumed him. He cries from the insults and torment he endures.

We know the wisecracks about the overly zealous church lady—the one about whom it is said, "She's there every time the church doors open."

Granted, overzealousness can be unhealthy. Yet being embarrassed about our faith is not good either. Inviting others to visit our community of faith, living out our faith, and sharing the good news of the gospel are our calling as Christians. So why do we shy away from zealously exhibiting evidence of God's presence in our lives? Are we afraid of being labeled "too religious for comfort"?

The psalmist struggled in his zeal for God. The apostle Paul said, "We are fools for the sake of Christ." Yet, without some degree of zeal, we are nothing but lukewarm Christians occasionally attending a little social group we call the church.

God, kick us into action. Ignite in us a fire for you that cannot be extinguished, a flame of faith that must be shared with zeal, love, tolerance, and compassion. Amen.

Spring cleaning comes each year, and with it come chaos and disruption. I'm happy for the order and cleanliness that come at the end, but I approach these tasks with resignation and not zeal! What a different picture we see when Jesus cleans house.

Jesus' disciples remembered that it was written, "Zeal for your house will consume me" (v. 17). The dictionary defines *zeal* as ardent interest in the pursuit of something. When the disciples see Jesus in action—whips fashioned, tables overturned, coins on the floor—it could not be clearer that Jesus is setting up a new order. It is no ordinary house cleaning. It is Jesus' first public act in John, and we are struck with how life with Jesus will upset the apple carts of our lives. As Jesus cleans house, we see that removing the barriers to life in God's community will take undiminished focus and commitment.

What needs overturning in our lives? Do we approach life in God's community with complacency? Do we accept comfortable pews over service to the world? Is our commitment to the kingdom of God all-consuming?

Lord, shake us from our complacency, and let us be consumed with zeal for the work of your kingdom. Amen.

*A*gricultural drought is when there isn't enough water for a crop to grow in a specific location although how much water is needed depends on the particular plant. The psalmist is certain that the water offered through the word of God is more than enough to produce a faithful life.

The either/or description of a faithful life in this psalm is a little unsettling. There are seasons in our faith when we are stricken with drought. At other times, we catch a glimpse of our place in the kingdom of God, and it can astound us. In whatever season of faith we are, we can give thanks that the God we worship is faithful in offering us what we need for life.

In the waters of baptism, God claims us and nourishes us with gifts of grace and forgiveness. What waters of grace feed your life? Where are signs of drought in your community that need God's life-affirming gifts?

Lord, in times of drought and joy, help us to trust that you offer us all that we need for life and faith. Amen.

*M*y youngest child died when she was a month old. For months after her death, my yearning to hold her again was overwhelming. This psalm, so open in its depiction of sorrow and longing, was my companion during those days.

During Joanna's short life, my church provided her and my family with every form of physical, emotional, and spiritual support. But my prayers were angry, and I was depressed. One day, I told a friend that I just couldn't say some of the words of hope and comfort that had so often come from my mouth. "That's OK," she said. "The church will say them for you."

The remembrance of the joyful praise of God with the worshiping community is a beacon of hope in the midst of the psalmist's despair. Even when I struggled with my feelings of anger and sorrow, my congregation claimed God's promises on my behalf. How do you experience your longing for God when life is difficult? How does your congregation stand with those in despair as a hopeful reminder of God's presence?

Lord, may our communities be a place of hope for those who feel despair. Amen.

There is no more potent symbol in the Bible than water. Moses parts the waters of the Red Sea. Naaman washes seven times in the Jordan River, and his leprosy is healed. Jesus is baptized with water, and he washes his disciples' feet. The story of creation begins with the wind of God sweeping over the face of the waters, and the Bible ends with this heartfelt invitation to come to the waters of life.

There is a country song from several years ago whose refrain is "[We] go through life parched and empty, standing knee deep in a river and dying of thirst." Christ's invitation is to drink deeply of the life that he offers, but we often choose to follow roads that cannot sustain our lives. We drink from the cup of narrow-mindedness, fear, or apathy, and it is no wonder that we sometimes feel that we are dying of thirst.

Christ invites us to come, follow him, and enter his kingdom, where justice rolls down like waters and peace flows like a river. In these waters is life abundant.

Lord, restore our dry and parched lives with your restorative living water. Amen.

There's a "just in case" mentality about the Samaritans. Sent by the Assyrians to live in Samaria after Israel's defeat, the new settlers bring with them a variety of religious gods and practices. But just in case that isn't enough, they are happy to worship Yahweh. If worshiping one god is good, worshiping more than one god must surely help them hedge their bets in this new land.

We are not that different from the Samaritans. We want to serve God alone, but in reality our lives are a mixture of worshiping God and hedging our bets by allegiance to other elements of our culture. We profess that the church is a place where all God's children are welcome, but the gods of prejudice keep us from truly welcoming all. We want to practice stewardship of God's gifts, but the gods of consumerism and greed seem to have more power over us than God's commands to share with the world.

We don't need a backup plan to help us navigate our lives. We worship a God whose gift and grace are sufficient for our every need.

Lord, may you alone be the focus of our praise and worship.
Amen.

The story of Jesus' encounter with the Samaritan woman at the well is one of my favorite stories. It is one of those frequent upside-down stories where Jesus engages with those least likely to be afforded respect in Jewish culture. But it isn't Jesus who gets most of my attention in this story; it is the woman. Despite her low status, she doesn't flinch from engaging Jesus in a kind of a theological question-and-answer session. She offers hope in the face of Jesus' words that "you worship what you do not know" (v. 22).

The Bible offers us the witness of Christ's life and ministry, but it is far from an advice column with answers for every question that confronts us. Like the woman, we don't know or understand all that we want to about God. Like Paul, we often see dimly. But this woman's questioning conversation with Jesus demonstrates that she learns. In her engagement in the conversation, she begins to understand. How do you engage Christ in the conversations of your life so that you grow in knowledge and faith?

Lord, open our minds and hearts to that which you want us to learn. Amen.

*W*hen my three-year-old granddaughter enters our garden, she sees her personal tomato patch, planted just for her eating pleasure. When I observe our garden, my mind conjures up endless hours at the stove canning tomato sauce. It's all in your perspective.

Jesus asks his disciples to get some perspective. Where they see a woman (and not a very reputable one at that) and a Samaritan, Jesus sees a person who wants to know more about him. When they want to focus on the minutiae of life, Jesus tells them to open their eyes and see what needs to be done in the world God loves. There's a whole world out there, he says, and it needs our attention.

Our perspective on life can limit us. Our political perspectives can keep us from talking with those who think differently. Our social perspectives keep our sight focused firmly on people just like us. Our theological perspectives sometimes keep us from seeing how God might be working. God asks us to change our perspective, see the world through God's eyes, and join God in his redemptive work for all people.

Lord, help us to see the world with your eyes and serve you faithfully in it. Amen.

*C*ome and see" is an invitation we've all received. "Mimi, come and see this bug!" my granddaughter exclaims. "Come and see the new picture on my wall," requests your friend. The invitation to share an experience requires something of us. We have to get up, move, change positions, and engage our bodies and minds in considering that which those issuing the invitation see.

We also sometimes need support in making sense of what we see. Andrew and Nathanael, receiving the invitation to come and see Jesus in action, respond with discipleship. The Samaritan woman, however, runs to her community and asks them to come and see in order to help her make sense of her encounter with Jesus. Can she trust what she has experienced? She wants others to help her on this journey to understanding.

Our communities can help move us to get up and follow Jesus and to consider where he might be leading us. They can also encourage us to recognize his claim on our lives. How does your church help you engage your body and soul in encountering Jesus? How do you encourage others around you to come and see Jesus?

Lord, thank you for those who invite us to come and see you. Amen.

One of my favorite hymns is "God of Our Life, through All the Circling Years." God's presence in our past, present, and future is a confident hope that runs through all three verses. At the end of the hymn, however, is a surprising phrase: "When we are strong, Lord, leave us not alone; Our Refuge be."

This hymn came to mind in reading Isaiah's message written to the kingdom of Judah during a time when they actually thought things were going pretty well. The nation seemed strong and prosperous. No wonder Isaiah had to keep hammering his points home. It is hard to hear the warnings about your choices in life if you think things are in pretty good shape and you think you can handle whatever life brings.

When life is at its most confusing, as well as when we feel strong, we need to remember that we hope in a trustworthy and loving God. The hope of God's presence in the world is not wishful thinking that all will be well with us. It is a confident expectation that God's will for the world can be trusted.

Lord, help us to put our hope in your strength and grace. Amen.

*W*hen Hurricane Isabel tore through my city in 2003, my husband and I found ourselves without power for three weeks. No street lights shone through the windows. Our battery supply ran out in the first week. Each night, far earlier than we were ready for it, complete darkness descended around us inside the house. It was eerie and, honestly, a little frightening.

The poetic description of God's creative acts in Genesis 1 testifies to God's intention for all created things to enjoy and be nourished by light. Plants grow. Seasons pass. By separating light and darkness, we are enabled to live more fully and see more clearly the wonders that God has created.

Jesus, the light of the world, comes to show us a world that darkness cannot overcome. Christ's light separates us from the darkness of our tendencies toward selfishness, pride, and apathy. Christ's light enables us to see the world as God sees it and to walk in that light as we seek to serve God. Thanks be to God for the marvelous gift of light.

Lord, enlighten us with the true light of life. Amen.

I have a friend whose son trains soldiers in escape techniques. Much of their training involves being blindfolded and put into hazardous situations that they must get out of without any light for guidance. Not surprisingly, many of the new soldiers panic in these training exercises. An unknown experience in complete darkness can be terrifying.

John 1 tells us that God's light came to shine forth in the darkness. In the life and words of Jesus, we have the clearest expression of what that light exposes. God's gift of light enables us to see brokenness so that we can seek wholeness, to recognize pain so we that we can engage in acts of healing. We can move in faith because we have the light of Christ to lead us. The Bible is full of stories in which nations and people close their eyes when confronted with God's light. In this passage from Exodus, the Israelites keep their eyes open and follow the pillar of light that God provides to safety.

In what ways has God's light illumined your walk of faith? Have there been particular times when you have felt God guiding you day and night?

Lord, help us to both live in and reflect your light. Amen.

*D*uring a recent visit, I heard my young granddaughter ask her mother if she could have a cookie. I clearly heard my daughter tell her that she would have to wait until supper. Soon, my granddaughter was snuggling up to me and asking me with innocent eyes if she could have a cookie. She didn't like the first answer, so she just went looking for another one!

The church is dealing with many big questions these days. What is marriage? Who can be ordained? What is our mission? Many of these questions frighten us or make us angry or leave us confused. The Pharisees show us how hard it is to see good news when we are only interested in looking at life in one way. The healed blind man doesn't respond in the way the Pharisees want, so they just go looking for others who will confirm their view of life.

What blinders do we wear when we look at the world? What practices might help you see God's activity in the world more clearly?

Lord, open our eyes that we might see you more clearly. Amen.

*A*lthough I was a very good student in high school, chemistry eluded me. My parents hired a gracious and patient woman who worked with me for many months, but understanding was slow and painful. So I have some sympathy with the Pharisees here. Learning something new is frequently difficult and frustrating!

In order to acquire any knowledge, no matter how challenging, one has to be open to actually learning something. Not only are the Pharisees not open to learning about Jesus; they are downright hostile to any understanding of him that differs from theirs. They may act as if they are genuinely curious with the questions they ask, but in reality, they are just looking for confirmation for what they think they already know.

Are we guilty of closing our minds to others whose experience of God and God's work might be different from ours? How can we balance the certainty of our convictions with the need to be open to the leading of God's spirit through all sorts of people?

Lord, help us to be willing to learn from the surprising ways that you work in the world. Amen.

I have no central vision in my right eye, and it occasionally affects my perception. Recently, I went to pick up my mother at the airport. As I gazed at the row of people filing up the long terminal corridor, I thought I recognized her. Waving happily, I was somewhat chagrined as the person I thought was my mother approached, and I realized I was waving at a twenty-something young woman. I was seeing, but not seeing!

Through the entire story of the man born blind, people have been slow to recognize Jesus. The Pharisees can't see him because of their preconceived notions of how God works. The parents, who should be leaping in joy over their son's amazing cure, are too afraid of the Pharisees even to attempt to look. The blind man, while acknowledging openly what Jesus did for him, takes a while to respond in worship.

Paul admits our reality when he speaks of the ways that we dimly view how God is working in our lives and in the world. We don't always see clearly, but God is present, always seeking to reveal God's goodness and grace. Keep your eyes open for the wonders you might see!

Lord, thank you for showing yourself to us. Amen.

When our granddaughter visited us recently, bedtime became something of an ordeal. When she admitted that she was scared of the dark, the solution was simple. We turned on a light and left it on all night. The fears that were too great for her to deal with in the dark disappeared in a strong light.

According to Scripture, light enables life to grow, guides our feet, illumines a path, or casts out fear. In John, the "light of the world" (v. 5) serves as revelation. God is revealed to us through Christ's life and teachings. Reflected in this light, we see who we are as children created in God's image. We are given the vision to see what walking in this light can mean for us and for the world. Christ's light serves as a mirror to how we are to live in faith in God's world.

Wherever the shadows of our lives and communities and nations are darkest, the Light of the World comes to show us how to live.

Lord, may the light of your life illumine our vision so that we see and follow you. Amen.

*L*ast summer, my congregation read *Take This Bread* together. In it, author Sara Miles describes her experience of walking into an Episcopal church and receiving communion for the first time. In the receiving of bread, she was changed; she recognized in receiving food a deep calling to feed others. For Miles, that meant opening a food program for the poor in San Francisco, placing the food to be distributed around the altar. Her encounter with the risen Christ through the bread and wine of the Lord's Supper fed a hunger of which she had not previously been aware.

Through the stuff of the earth—barley loaves and fish—Jesus satisfied the hunger of those who gathered around him. There is no reason to expect that God would not also choose to use our earthbound, ordinary contributions to help speak to the many kinds of hunger that exist in our world.

What hunger do you perceive? What gifts have you been given to feed that hunger? Blessed by God's abundant grace, your simple gifts can be a means by which Christ's nourishment can be offered to those who hunger.

Lord, satisfy our hunger for a life lived in communion with you.
Amen.

*F*ear does strange things to people. When we fear we don't have enough, we hoard what we have. When we fear relationships, we shut ourselves off from human companionship. When we fear the future, we find it hard to live fully. In the midst of frightening realities, overwhelmed by tasks that sap our strength (try rowing four miles in the midst of a strong headwind!), consumed by work that seems as if it will never end, God comes to us. "It is I; do not be afraid," Jesus says (v. 20).

God does not promise that we will not face frightening situations. We will face our mortality. We may face financial uncertainty. We may face the loss of a marriage or watch the self-destructive choices of a friend. But God comes to us—in words of Scripture, in the comforting presence of a friend, in the bread and cup—and tells us that God's grace is stronger than the fears that assail us. God is with us. Keeping our eyes on Christ and holding on to the promise of God's presence, we keep moving toward a safe and firm shore.

Lord, help us to move beyond our fears to faith in you. Amen.

The word *eternal* is frequently used to describe what is endless, what goes on forever. Jesus tells us that God wants to give us eternal life. But what distinguishes this life is not how long it goes on but certain realities. In the eternal life God gives us, we will not be hungry. We will never be turned away. We will be raised to life.

Eternal life is offered to us in the present tense. The gift that is eternal life is experienced by knowing and following Christ who reveals it to us. God calls us to that life now, even as God promises the life that will be. Nourished by the bread of life and following the light of world, we can accept God's gift of the abundant life now.

Christ's resurrection assures us that God is stronger than death and that our life continues with God after death. But the question we should be asking ourselves is not "Will I live eternally?" We need to ask if we are living now.

Lord, help us to live the gift of eternal life that you offer us now. Amen.

*I*n a class for families who were preparing their children to participate in the Lord's Supper for the first time, the leaders held a bread-baking gathering for the participants on a Saturday morning. After flour, yeast, and water had been mixed together and the bread bowls were covered, families learned about communion. On returning to the kitchen, a rambunctious four-year-old was given the task of removing the cloth cover from the bowl that held the rising dough. "Mama!" he exclaimed at the growing lump. "This bread is alive!"

In our sharing at the Lord's Table, we make our claims that the bread is alive. Whether our recipe makes a risen loaf or a flat wafer, the bread becomes the life of Christ in us and for us. In sharing the bread, in remembering Christ's life and ministry, our lives are shaped by the very one who nourishes us.

In my church, bread that remains after communion is used to make sandwiches for the hungry in our community. It is but one response we make to having received life-giving nourishment at God's table. How do you respond to this gracious gift?

Lord, may we be fed by your living bread so our lives show your love. Amen.

*T*his teaching is too hard. Who can listen to it?" We'd like faith to be simple, easy to understand. We'd like it to demand little and offer many things.

The followers of Jesus had just experienced a satisfying banquet. That's easy. Then Jesus, turning from bread, makes them think about real bread, the Bread of Life. We don't want to wrestle with things that aren't readily apparent. We don't want to consider things like evil in a world where a good God is sovereign, suffering in the life of a faithful disciple, or life that comes not from our good works but from the Living Bread. We turn to other things—entertainment, conversation, sports. We don't want to listen. But suppose, as Jesus implies, there are yet harder things. Suppose that we don't understand our faith completely or that we deaden our hearts when we meet what we don't like and don't want to hear.

Two promises bring hope to the believers. These difficult words bring God's life-giving Spirit. It is God's work that enables us to listen, learn, and obey hard things.

Lord, through your Spirit, enable us to follow you even when it is not easy. Amen.

*S*everal years ago, I was involved in planning a youth pilgrimage to South Dakota for a group of bright and interesting young people. The pilgrimage was to culminate in confirmation. Most of these young people had grown up and been active in the church their entire lives. When they returned, all but one of them felt they could not honestly answer the questions about Jesus asked of those wishing to become members of the church. They opted not to be confirmed. It was a sobering moment. Had we failed to demonstrate in our life together who we believed Christ to be?

"Who do people say that I am?" Jesus asks his disciples in Mark. In this chapter from John's Gospel, Peter doesn't respond to a question. He responds to an opportunity. He has an opportunity to turn away from Jesus, to leave behind the difficult things that Jesus is teaching. But he can't. In the presence of Christ, he sees something from which he cannot turn away.

Who is Jesus to you? How do you come to know the claims that Jesus has on you? And how does the church share that vision of Christ with others?

Lord, help us turn to you as we seek to live into faith. Amen.

*N*ever to be hungry. Never to yearn for healing or love or contentment. Jesus says that believing in him means no more hunger, no painful thirst. Those who hear him expect real bread. Jesus is telling us something a little different—this bread does not merely satisfy physical hunger. God has sent Jesus to be the bread that nourishes our life's relationship with God. It is the mark of God's unending presence with us.

We need no sign—no manna from heaven, no miracles—to assure us, says Jesus. And there are no guarantees of comfort, no assurances that our old ideas won't be challenged, that our faith won't wobble as we go through life. Jesus does not make that promise but instead calls to us to stay with him and trust that God abides with us. It's a little like closing your eyes and on a hot, hot day falling into a pool to revel in the cool water. Surround yourself, sink into, abide in the presence of God.

Fill us, Lord, with assurance in your presence. Amen.

$\mathcal{J}$ust tell him what he wants to hear." Four hundred "yes" men are ready to send the country to war, but the king wants to know if there is any prophet with another view. Micaiah promises to speak only what God has put in his mouth. But he gives the king the same advice! And he says that it's all a deliberate lie. How to entice the enemy? Get the rumor mill going. Spread the word from unnamed sources. Publish codes to these prophecies, and feed the enemy misinformation.

Is this how God works? Is a thief used to catch a thief? A cheat, to catch a cheat? This Scripture challenges our tendency to believe that God follows our rules. It is just not that simple. God claims and speaks for truth. It is truth we don't always want to hear and one that demands obedience, even in the face of chaos and uncertainty. There are times when trusting God seems to be a pretty risky enterprise. But all we can do is trust that the Shepherd will indeed bring us through.

Be with us, Lord, in all the dark places we must walk. Amen.

*I*f you have traveled to Jordan and visited Mt. Nebo, you have seen an amazing view. Looking northwest, you see the Jordan rift valley and the Dead Sea. A huge expanse of land—and you stand there imagining the feelings Moses might have had. The Lord showed him this land, saying, "This is it." But you, Moses, can only grasp it with your eyes. You will not enter it. What you can do is pass some of the spirit and power of your authority to Joshua, who will lead the people as your successor.

Then imagine Joshua, chosen by God to lead the children of Israel across the river and into this land. What might it be like to have the entire burden of this huge project shifted now onto your shoulders—to take up the responsibility to win the wars, send out the spies, and resolve the tribal arguments? For Joshua, and for us, there is comfort in the truth expressed in James Russell Lowell's poem that "behind the dim unknown, standeth God within the shadow, keeping watch above His own."

Guide us, Lord, and give us strength to serve. Amen.

*W*ho better to shepherd the people, asks the psalmist, than a shepherd? This psalm recounts all that God has done for the errant children of Israel. Over and over, God brings them through trials, guides them through the wilderness, and answers their doubts and complaints with rich generosity. Our God created all things good. God also sees to creation's needs. God provides. When the wandering Israelites complain about food, God rains down manna. And they still complain.

God is faithful still. Though they provoked God's anger, they were not forever abandoned. God chose the small tribe of Judah and looked to Mount Zion, a favored place, a thin place where heaven and earth nearly touch. From there, God chose David, a shepherd, to care for the wandering children. God chose one not of high and noble birth, not of wealth or connection, but of true heart and great gifts of leadership.

This is the great story we are called to tell. When our daily worries seem to overwhelm, the sure truth of God fills us with the assurance that we, too, have been given what we need.

Remind us, Lord, that you daily provide for us. Amen.

*O*h, there are times when the Lord seems far away, times when comfort is far distant, times when we feel vulnerable to pain and loss. Hear my voice, Lord, my whispers, my quiet cries for help. Death touches us all, but there are those times when no lament can catch our suffering. Relationships are severed by death. Sickness breaks our bodies; age weakens us. These things separate us from those we love and threaten to separate us from God. The psalms of lament give us words to speak from the depths. Where is God in this? Where is God in this disaster when my soul knows no comfort? I cannot pray. There is no balm for my grief.

Many have found the Lord to be their refuge; God heard their cries. It is a constant in the Gospels—Jesus hears and sees the needs of the people. He is there with them. The Lord is indeed our shepherd, is indeed our strength and shield. All of us together may find saving refuge in God's loving care.

Together we plead for your presence, Lord. Be with us. Amen.

There is such power in this psalm. The psalmist calls God to come with might. The call is spoken from strength, from a strong person who is not about to give up: "Stir up your might; come and save us! Don't stand there—we are here fighting for you! Come, join us in the struggle! We have had our fill of tears, but now we are in the thick of it."

Here is a writer who says to God, "Let your face shine" when we know from Scripture that none of us can bear to see the face of God and live. If God is for us, said Paul, no one can be against us. "We are strong, but we are strong because you, Lord, have made us so for your purposes." Too often, we underestimate our gifts—are we really, truly able to accomplish the task we have been given? We have to brave the struggle and trust that God has indeed provided for us, restored us to strength—indeed, made us more than conquerors through the One who loves us.

Lead us, Good Shepherd, to fullness of life, to peace and joy. Amen.

*W*e aren't sheep. We don't go along with the herd, the pack, the crowd. We have more sense than that. Surely we think for ourselves. Jesus' sheepish metaphor is pretty hard to get our heads around in this very modern world. We would rather not be dependent on anyone or ruled by anyone. But that isn't the point of Jesus' story. It is not *about* the sheep. It is about the shepherd.

The shepherd calls each and every sheep, protects each one, guides each one away from harm, and sees to it that the keeper of the fold knows whose sheep come through the gate. The shepherd does all this. For the sheep, for those so guided, the task is to get to know and to love the voice that calls us by name. The path we take to follow that voice is an incredibly hard one. There are dangers and frustrations. There must surely be an easier way into the sheepfold. The task is hard—to follow the voice we love even when it takes us the long way round.

Lord, lead us wherever the path leads. Amen.

Shepherds, thieves, hired hands. Three choices. With whom do you trust your life?

Thieves come to kill, steal, and destroy. Hired hands do not own the sheep, so when faced with danger, they abandon the flock.

If the shepherd is the only choice, why do we give our lives away to thieves and hired hands? How is it that we allow ourselves to be deceived by other voices? Thieves sneak around the edges of your life. Have you ever been aware of their presence? Have you noticed how their voices have attempted to drown out the voice of the good shepherd?

The hired hand may be more difficult to recognize, for he looks like a shepherd on the surface. But a hired hand will not lay down his life. Have you followed a hired hand down a path that leads to despair instead of hope? To death instead of life?

If so, then stop where you are and listen. Really listen. The shepherd's voice is clear and true, and in it you will find rest. Run to the shepherd's side; run to the side of the one who has laid down his life for you.

Good Shepherd, thank you for walking before me on the path that leads to life. Amen.

*W*hen we refer to "Christ's suffering," the scene on the cross comes to mind. That is, of course, the primary suffering referred to in this passage. Christ's death on the cross was not only wrought with horrific physical pain but also with emotional, mental, and spiritual anguish. Yet on some level the hours on the cross were only a glimpse into the suffering Christ must have known.

Each day of his life must have been difficult. How he must have suffered each time someone turned away from the truth, each time someone turned away from his healing. How he must have anguished as he awoke each day to the awareness that he could not take away human suffering.

When we suffer from injustice, from oppression, or from illness, Christ shares in our suffering. We can take comfort in knowing that there is no pain we can experience that Christ has not known. Abuse. Injustice. Disrespect. Hunger. Loneliness. Despair.

But what does it mean for *us* to share in *Christ's* suffering? We share Christ's pain when we sacrifice our wants to stand against abuse, injustice, disrespect, hunger, loneliness, despair. We have the potential to bear Christ's suffering in a myriad of choices we face each day.

Lord Jesus, show us what it means to share in your suffering.
May we never forget what you endured on our behalf. Amen.

*C*hildren watch their parents, their teachers, older brothers or sisters, and the big kids in the neighborhood. They watch, and they learn. Sometimes they pick up things their parents wish they had missed!

Jesus says that he watches God, much like a child watches a parent. By watching God, Christ learns what to do, learns what he *can* do. He doesn't say he listens for God to *tell* him what to do; he says that he does whatever he "*sees* the Father doing" (v. 19). Can we ever be reminded of that enough? Our actions speak volumes. Even Christ looks to God. God teaches the Son through powerful example.

So we stay connected to the stories of Christ's life on earth. We return again and again to the One who walked before us. In his encounters with outsiders, the displaced, the proud, the lost, we can learn who we are called to be. But we have to watch in order to learn.

Great Teacher, open our eyes to the truth of Christ's life. May we have the courage to watch and learn. Amen.

$\mathcal{D}$o not be astonished," Jesus says (v. 28). Do not be astonished to discover that it is Christ who holds the gift of life. Do not be astonished that the Son of God holds the same power and authority as the Father. Do not be astonished, but believe.

Again we wonder, how will we recognize the Son of God? By his voice! A voice that will call the dead to life, just as it called to Lazarus. Jesus' voice is not limited by anyone or anything. His voice contains the power to restore life to those who hear it and answer.

We should not be amazed by this. As Paul reminds us in Romans 8:38–39, "I am convinced that neither death, nor life, nor angels, nor rulers, nor things present, nor things to come, nor powers, nor height, nor depth, nor anything else in all creation, will be able to separate us from the love of God in Christ Jesus our Lord." Nothing can separate us. Not the evil that we have done. Not our deafness. Not death. Nothing can separate us. Jesus calls us to life.

God of Life, you have called us by name, and we are yours. You have called us from despair to hope, from death to life. Attune our ears to your powerful voice. Amen.

*C*urious people sought Jesus, determined to discover if this mysterious person could really be the son of God. Those who were gathered at the temple on this particular day believed he was trying to keep his identity a secret. They thought he was intentionally holding back, so they asked him, "Who are you?" They did not want a parable; they wanted a plain answer. Jesus had been offering the simple truth through his actions: healing, feeding, comforting, restoring. These works, done in God's name, proclaimed his identity at every turn.

How heartbroken Jesus must have felt when he said to them, "I have told you, but you do not believe. Why can you not imagine me as a good shepherd?" he asked. "What prevents you from believing that I came to offer *you* healing and sustenance, green pastures and safe passage through the dangerous paths? If you could only believe, then you could rest without fear." What was it that held them back? Their discomfort with a God who looks like a shepherd rather than a king? What is it that holds me back? What holds me back from resting in the knowledge that Christ is my good shepherd and in Him is the source of life?

Good Shepherd, source of life and truth, thank you for welcoming me even when I come with doubts and fears and questions. Amen.

*N*avigating in the darkness can be challenging for the sighted. We strain to use the light available. We can't see the step ahead. We might miss the turn that comes up too suddenly. Even the most familiar path can be hazardous. Shadows shift, and recognizable objects appear strange. Darkness can be treacherous.

Jesus is concerned with the darkness and with those who dwell in it. Those who wish to see him dead walk in darkness. They have no light in them because they have rejected the One who is the Light. Jesus does not fear what they may do to him, for the light will shine in the darkness, and the darkness will not overcome it. Living in darkness means living without warmth, living in fear, living in confusion.

Walking in physical darkness may lead to little more than a stubbed toe or a bruised knee, but living in spiritual darkness is much more dangerous.

Light of the World, shine upon us to light our path. In your light, we do not have to be afraid of the world around us. To live in your light is to know your truth and peace, which the darkness cannot overcome. Amen.

Questions of life and death confront us. Lazarus' life and death. Jesus' life and death. The disciples' lives and deaths.

Lazarus has died. Jesus has allowed Lazarus to die so that the disciples might believe that he has power over life and death. Restoring Lazarus to life is no more difficult than awakening him, which is how Jesus describes it. Like a parent waking a sleeping child, Jesus will gently rouse Lazarus from death.

The disciples hear the words, not the meaning. Soon they will see Lazarus restored. Soon they will stand in awe at God's power. Still it will not be enough to fortify them when it is Jesus' time to die. They will cower in fear that the One who raised Lazarus will not return to life but leave them like sheep without a shepherd.

And what about Thomas, who in his incomplete understanding was still willing to follow Jesus into death? There are worse things than to be like this disciple, who did not fear accompanying Christ, no matter where the path might end.

Christ, we praise your name. You hold power over death. We thank you that we need not fear, for our lives are in your hands. Amen.

We don't know why it takes Jesus so long to go to Lazarus, why he waits until Lazarus is dead. He has his reasons, and he trusts Martha to understand. Martha is naturally upset with Jesus for not having arrived sooner. She is comfortable enough to let him know she's not pleased, but faithful enough to believe he still can do something. It's an interesting turn, because when we meet Martha in Luke's Gospel, Jesus tells her not to be so distracted! In John's account, we begin to understand God's power over death and the promise of eternal life.

In their conversation, Martha gets it—she is a model for faith and trust for all of us. Her brother has died, and even in her grief, when Jesus tells her that all who believe in him will live— even after death—she affirms her belief in Jesus as the Messiah, the Son of God.

There are times when we need to be Martha for someone else—to claim the promise of eternal life for all who believe in Jesus, the resurrection and the life.

Sovereign God, whose power is unending, even over death,
thank you for the hope you give us through your son. Amen.

*I*f I don't do it, it won't get done." "I don't have time to show you how to do it." Sound familiar? When do you stop and rest? We keep doing, refusing help, not teaching others to share in whatever the task, and we're exhausted. Kind of like Moses. It's probably safe to say that more than a few of us need the wise counsel of Jethro in our lives!

Time in the wilderness is elemental in forming the Israelites as God's people. They have to unlearn who they were in Egypt—and learn new ways of working and living. If Moses does not teach others to share leadership, what will happen in the future? One aspect of being a good leader is developing and nurturing new leaders. None of us is indispensible.

How do you model a balanced life for your family or co-workers? What do you do to develop leadership skills in others at home, at church, or at work?

Creator God, instill in us the desire not just to do our work but to share our skills with others. Help us to seek a balance between work and Sabbath time. Amen.

*W*hen things are difficult and God seems far away, it's tempting to believe in something we can see or touch. The siren call of our culture points to many possible idols: electronic gadgets, sports, work, clothing, food, cars, and other consumer goods. But none of these things bring true satisfaction. None of them can make a covenant to be our God, to be present in all times and places. None of them will love us. Certainly, none are worthy of our trust. And yet we often choose something other than God.

Our faith becomes another item on our "to do" lists. Attending church so we can check it off the list isn't sufficient. To turn from whatever we create as an idol, we need to be more intentional. We need the help and support of our faith community.

What is the idol that gets between you and God? Who can you make a covenant with to keep you on the way?

We are so grateful that you do not give up on us, Lord. Help us not to be stiff-necked but to worship you alone. Amen.

*H*ave you seen the "Wash Away Your Sins" soap? It comes in all the regular soap options, but this soap is formulated to soothe guilty consciences and kill sins on contact. Oh, and as a bonus, it smells divine. All you need is the right kind of soap, and you are good to go! For tactile people, that physical action can be a tangible way of releasing sin.

In Christ, our sins have been washed away. In that confidence, we need to examine ourselves honestly, searching out the wrongs we have done and the hurts we have caused. We might be able to hide them from our family or friends, but not from God. God already knows—the confession is for us. Any assurance of grace rings hollow when we do not truly acknowledge our sins. No cleansing can be complete without washing all the dirt away.

What is it you think you are hiding? Why are you afraid of confession? When you confess to God, you can be assured that God in Christ has forgiven all your sins, and you won't even have had to buy special soap.

Compassionate God, thank you for washing away our sins in the water of baptism and for continuing to forgive our sins. Amen.

*A*t times when asked a question, we respond without thinking first. It could be a truthful answer, but not particularly tactful or caring. The same thing can happen when we speak in anger. The words come rushing out, full of emotion, before we can rein them in. Words are powerful. They can be used to honor and respect, to care and love, or to inflict harm and fear. Careless or hateful words can leave deep scars. It's not only what we say but how we say it.

Speaking the truth from our hearts means not letting words spill from our mouths without thought. It means clamping shut when we are about to say something better left unsaid. Do we really need to speak out loud the unkind thought, the rumor, the sarcastic comment? How might things change if we looked for things to compliment instead of disparage; if we spoke even difficult truths gently and with kindness?

Lord God, may our words be a blessing to you and to others. Amen.

Through the death and resurrection of our Lord Jesus Christ, we have been saved by grace! There will never be any better news! Yet while we eagerly share the news of a great sale or speak glowingly of our children's accomplishments, we are reluctant to talk about Jesus' life, ministry, death, and resurrection. To hear some Christians talk, Jesus is no different from others who suffer or endure persecution. To understand Jesus' significance, however, we have to consider the whole story of his ministry, teachings, and miracles. More personally, we understand the power of Jesus when we hear how God is at work in one another's lives, how we experience God's love and grace.

Sharing the good news doesn't mean getting in people's faces or shouting at them. It does mean looking for opportunities to share our faith by deed or word, holding to our principles, and living as those who know God's grace. It means being patient and kind. It means looking the homeless person in the eye and saying hello. We rightly regard all God's children with dignity.

Gracious God, may my words and actions reflect your presence in my life. Amen.

$\mathcal{J}$esus' teachings are difficult to obey. Take for example the instructions to go through the narrow gate and to walk the more difficult road. Jesus knew our preference for ease and aversion to hardship. Haven't we all, at some point, sought the easier road? It might be expedient, but it might also be in conflict with our values and who we profess to be.

Sometimes we get lost when we take the easy road. Conversely, walking the difficult road can be instructive and can deepen our faith—giving us new insight into ourselves and our God.

The call to take the hard road isn't meant to be punitive, and it may make us uneasy. Jesus is pretty clear that we are not called to do what is easy but to do what is right. What are the bumps you have encountered on your journey? What made travel difficult? We have to remember that nowhere does it say that being a Christian is easy.

Guide our hearts and feet to the follow the road you call us to follow. Amen.

$\mathcal{J}$ustice runs through each of this week's readings as a common thread, but it is not immediately apparent how John 14 fits the justice theme. We usually hear, "I go to prepare a place for you" (v. 3) during the Easter season. Perhaps we've shared these verses with a loved one nearing death, but it is not a passage that comes to mind when we talk about justice. For that reason, you might find it illuminating to skim through all of the designated Scripture passages for the week. Look for the justice thread in each reading, and then take a moment to wonder how John 14 fits into the larger fabric.

The first thing you may notice is the emphasis on God's brand of justice and the failure of earthly institutions to live up to God's standards. Those who pursue justice can remain true to God's version of justice only by knowing God. And this is where we see the tie to John 14. Like Jesus' disciples, we who desire to live justly must ask, "How can we know the way?" (v. 5). And in response to our question comes the invitation to follow Christ who is "the way, the truth, and the life" (v. 6). In following Christ we find a pattern for enacting God-fashioned justice.

Just God, guide our steps on the path toward your righteousness. Amen.

A Quiet Recess in the Warm Grass

In some ways it is impossible to compare the law prescribed in Deuteronomy to the laws that govern our place and time. On the other hand, it's mortifying to discover the malicious nature of people across the centuries that makes these laws necessary.

In our day, just as in Moses' day, there are an unreasonable number of people prone to go to court to settle disputes without any effort to make amends outside of the courts. There is a cultural norm to "make someone pay." When we allow God's justice to guide our lives, however, we are less likely to see ourselves as victims and more likely to see the accused as one of God's beloved creatures.

God's covenant justice is carried forward in the New Testament when Paul instructs Christians, "If it is possible, as far as it depends on you, live at peace with everyone." God's plan for justice is essentially a plan for peace; our lives most align with God's will when we seek the interests of others above our own.

Loving God, help us to see our adversaries for who they truly are—your beloved children. Amen.

The psalmist claims that any authority held by an earthly ruler originates from God. If all earthly rulers accepted the psalmist's claim, then we would see some fundamental changes in how countries are governed.

God has a radical plan for peace! If the world's economic and political leaders—and yes, religious leaders—would acknowledge the One in whom all authority resides, then they would deal more fairly and more compassionately with the people who depend on their leadership. Christians cannot wait for the trickle-down effect in this one instance. Even if we are not in positions of power, we can make a difference in the lives of those in need. Why? Because nothing indicates a greater alignment with the heart of God than lovingly extending relief to those who need it.

There are a number of ways to make a difference, but one effort that is commonly overlooked is prayer. As Israel's prayer book, the Psalms offer us a pattern and a guide for our prayers. As our prayers take root in us, a pattern for living will also emerge.

O God, guide our prayers and our behaviors. Lead us in the way of peace and justice. Amen.

*N*othing stirs up God's anger more fiercely than our lack of concern for those who are in need. Scripture witnesses to God's compassion for the downtrodden. Compassion for the poor was a requirement of God's covenant with Israel and written into the law of Moses. God intended that everyone, especially the wealthy and powerful, would have a part in caring for every other member of the community.

We know from reading Isaiah and other prophets that Israel's failure to care for the poor signals a rebellious attitude toward God and the covenant. Isaiah 10:1–4 is but one Old Testament example of God's urgent plea for Israel to cease oppression of the poor.

The urgency of the message is reborn in Jesus' preaching. In Luke 4 Jesus tells the crowd, "The Spirit of the Lord . . . has anointed me to proclaim good news to the poor" (v. 18). As Christians desiring to live by God's word, we seek to love and protect the poor and the needy in our midst. We demonstrate our love for God every time we love "the least of these" (Matthew 24:40).

O God, help us see the poor and needy among us with new eyes. Help us love them with a compassionate and active love. Amen.

*H*ave you ever been unfairly treated—perhaps by an arrogant doctor, an unethical landlord, or a lecherous employer? Most people can probably confess to feeling powerless in the face of someone who abused his or her position of authority. It would really feel good to exact revenge on that person, to feel so powerful that we would never be mistreated again.

There are legitimate avenues in which we can pursue retribution. In addition to whatever official channels are at our disposal, the Psalms teach us another way to feel powerful: Bring all circumstances to the Lord in prayer. In every situation we can count on God to bring consolation and comfort.

"In you, O Lord, I take refuge" (v. 1). Like the psalmist who pleads for a safe place, we look to God to be a guest room where we can retreat.

In the solitude of prayer, we find our safe place, our refuge, and true power.

Loving God, empower me to trust you in all circumstances. Amen.

*B*elieving in a just and faithful God gives us assurance that when we confess our sin, God eagerly extends grace to us. God's mercy is everlasting. Even before we utter a cry of confession, God is ready and waiting with a loving response.

Although God guides and directs our lives, we are prone to sin. All is not lost should we stumble. There is a provision for failure. God lovingly helps get us back on course.

A Scottish faith statement puts it this way: "But the [children] of God . . . sob and mourn when they find themselves tempted to do evil; and, if they fall, rise again with earnest and unfeigned repentance. They do these things, not by their own power, but by the power of the Lord Jesus, apart from whom they can do nothing" (Scots Confession, 1560).

God holds high standards for righteousness, yet we are not asked to do the impossible. More importantly, we are not left to our own devices. God guides and guards our every step. We have only to listen. Quiet your heart, even in this moment, and hear God say, "This is the way; walk in it."

Holy God, set us on the right path. And if we should stumble, restore us by your mercy and grace in Jesus Christ. Amen.

*W*e can only imagine how it breaks God's heart when we stumble, but all of those failures fade into oblivion in the light of those moments when we get it right. Moses' song resounds with the gratitude of one who has known God's love, grace, forgiveness, and provision.

Read verses 1–4 out loud, or put them to a tune if you can. How do these lyrics resonate with your song of praise? What other songs of praise are familiar to you?

Notice how praise lifts your spirits and distracts you from the worries that can drag you down.

Yes, there are problems in the world and difficulties in our lives. But in the midst of it all, can you proclaim the name of the Lord? Will you ascribe greatness to our God? Yes! Because we serve an awesome God. At the end of the day, does anything else really matter?

God, give me a song of praise in my heart and on my lips. Amen.

The directives in Exodus are not rocket science. They are pretty basic, things our mothers taught us:

"If you can't say something nice about someone, don't say anything at all."

"Don't tell lies."

"Help those in need."

The ideas are simple, but living them can be so, so hard.

Why? Often it is simply a matter of wanting our way. Other times we just don't like someone, or, worse, we kind of enjoy the troubles of others and so gossip about them. Even more difficult, we are, at times, afraid of others, of "the alien."

But God doesn't ask us to fix all wrongs here or live with perfection. God asks us to live with compassion toward others; to see the humanity of those around us; to act with the heart of one who knows hurt. We are to help others even when we don't like them. We are to consider the hurt gossip does before we speak. We are to remember our isolation and pain, our experience of being an alien, before we oppress others.

God, give me a heart of compassion, that I might extend your mercy to those in need of grace. Amen.

*W*hew! That is one angry God. The wrath expressed in these lines is full-blown, making us want to shy away. However, truth can't be avoided.

Our world is testament enough to Ezekiel's words: bankers receive enormous bonuses, even while the taxpayers bail out their businesses; an enormous oil company neglects safety measures and refuses to take responsibility for the unprecedented disaster that resulted; political leaders argue over everything while two wars drag on endlessly. All while the people suffer.

God seeks those who will "repair the wall and stand in the breach" (v. 30) today. We cannot fix everything. But we are called to speak up, to vote, to participate. Simply by participating in our church, we contribute because our churches house the homeless, fund missionaries, and send groups to work in the community. All of this helps repair the wall; by these actions we stand in the breach. God seeks us there. Let God find us active, giving, and present.

God, help me to stand in the breach where I find it, bringing your grace and truth to the world. Amen.

The litany of sinful activity is long in this passage, swirling before us, stirring in our minds, ringing in our ears. At first glance, it seems far-fetched, but when phrased another way, perhaps it is not so far-fetched after all: stealing, murdering, adultery, lying, our focus on anything but God. The swirl of sin adds up today just as it did in biblical times. Our contemporary swirl may look a little different: hustling after money, overscheduling our time, embroidering the truth, focusing on outward appearance rather than inner vitality.

God seems to be saying to us, "Stop. Just stop. Come to my house and sit quietly. Don't talk; don't justify; don't fix; don't give me your money. Just stop; sit with me; listen; and let me be enough." And with a simple pause to experience the divine, the swirl can stop. And we are whole.

God of stillness, you call me from the chaos to be still before you, to enjoy you, and to live in you. Help me, this day, to live in you rather than in the rush and worry of this world. Amen.

"Deliver me, O LORD, from evildoers!" cries the psalmist (v. 1). They seem to be everywhere for the psalmist. There seems to be no end to their warmongering; their arrogant, violent, gossiping ways. Crying against the wicked may give vent to the psalmist's fears, but it does nothing to bring peace or joy to God.

Rest in the knowledge that God hears supplications and covers the head in the day of battle. God wants better for us than to live in fear. Somewhere, deep inside, the psalmist is reminded that comfort comes only from God.

We live in a constantly, quickly changing world. It can feel frightening, even threatening, but God is a constant presence, sure and steady: "O LORD, my Lord, my strong deliverer . . ." (v. 7). When we live in this knowledge, we have little to fear, especially from those we perceive to be evildoers.

O God of steadiness, comfort me when I am fearful. Help me remember your constancy that I may not fear people I do not understand, situations that seem uncertain, or places where I feel lost. You, O God, are my strong deliverer. Amen.

*U*nless you change and become like children . . . ," says Jesus (v. 3). When reared in a safe, caring environment, children tend to trust their parents, trust that they are provided for, trust that they are deeply and profoundly loved. This frees them for the important work of childhood: to learn and grow.

If we approach God with the same childlike trust—that we will be tenderly taken care of, that God genuinely wants good for us, that we are deeply loved and profoundly forgiven—how might we live differently? It frees us to explore, to try things, to live without fear, and, perhaps most important, to give to those around us.

How might we receive God's love and grace if we trusted as innocently as children trust their parents? How might we regard other people if we knew, as surely as young children, that God wants the most profound good for us? Could we release some of our fears? Could we find a more generous spirit?

Dear God, you tenderly care for me, nurture me, comfort me. May I just as tenderly give that love to those around me. Amen.

*A*pparently, a faithful life requires more than going to church, going to church, going to church. Jeremiah declares that faithfulness requires acting justly with one another. We need to be fair to the alien, the orphan, and the widow. We need to stop being so distracted by other "gods." Our relationships with other people have an effect on our relationship with God.

This message is repeated throughout Scripture, reminding us that a life of faith isn't simply about going to the temple. It is about loving God and loving others as ourselves. We are to treat other people, other creatures, even ourselves with care, respect, and equity. When we live this way, God dwells in us. We don't need to go constantly to the temple, to the temple, to the temple. We become the temple of the Lord as God dwells in us and we dwell in the living God.

Living God, make room in my heart to care for others. Make room in my heart that you might live in me. Amen.

*W*e like to overthink things, don't we? Here we have a simple directive: Love God; love your neighbor; love yourself; and you're going to live a full, rich life.

The lawyer wants to wrangle with the minutiae, to figure it out, to put every little thing in order. So Jesus tells the man a story because there is nothing like a good story for getting to the simple truth.

And that simple truth? Be a good neighbor; show mercy. The lawyer is busy figuring it out, parsing the definition of neighbor when Jesus is asking for action: show mercy. The lawyer is thinking, "Do I have to love everybody? What about that illegal immigrant over there? What about that smelly homeless guy? What about that brilliant rival who lives in the big house and looks like she has everything? Do I have to show them all mercy?"

Jesus keeps it simple. The answer is yes. Show mercy; love God; love your neighbor; love yourself. And you will live in ways you never imagined because all that figuring out was holding you back from joy.

Wondrous God, free me from my need to get a handle on everything and to narrow my definitions. Free me to embrace people and your world with love, mercy, and joy. Amen.

Y ou shall not. . . . I am the LORD." Between these words come important instructions. In our imperfection, we need God's rules to keep us in covenant community with God and one another. We need to be reminded again and again of how God wants us to live.

God calls us to love neighbor as self; to hold the poor, powerful, stranger, and friend to the same standards of justice. But in real life, our system of civil and criminal laws doesn't seem to connect with these commands. What's a Christ follower to do?

Verse 37 makes it clear: "You shall keep all my statutes and all my ordinances, and observe them: I am the LORD." This means our actions and words will set us apart from or in opposition to earthly statutes. I don't know about you, but for me it's a constant struggle to remember that God is God, and I am not.

Lord of all creation, I pray for the strength to live as you command; to follow your rules; to show through my actions as well as my words a love of neighbor, stranger, friend, and self. Amen.

*R*eading this passage, I get dizzy from all the turning around. God's people followed the rules; then they didn't; then they did; then they didn't. I imagine Jeremiah had a hard time keeping up as the people repented, then sinned again, then repented— of course, until God seems to have had it.

I remember feeling this way when my sons tested my patience as they learned to make their way in the world. "That's what happens when (insert inappropriate behavior or unkind action)" was part of the litany of each day, it seemed. I wondered if they would ever learn.

We are not off the hook as far as turning our lives around again and again as we seek to live as God's people. There are consequences. Yes, we have the promise of God's eternal love and salvation. But that doesn't mean we don't have to practice making "U-turns" as we focus living as the God of the Universe calls us to live.

Turn our hearts to You, God, and teach us that repentance is a continual way of life. Amen.

*H*ave you ever been as honest and self-assured in your praying as Nehemiah? Look at the prayer: an address to God, then a confession on behalf of the one praying and his kin. Nehemiah reminds God—as if God needed reminding—of the promise made to Moses and asks God to bless him as God blessed Moses. Then there's a twist at the end—a funny little reminder that he just happened to be a cupbearer to the king, a person of some consequence.

We are fools to think that our earthly status provides any sort of protection or exercises any influence with God when it comes to our tendency to sin and fall short. What matters is our confession of sin and our willingness to do something about it: like returning to God, head bowed and heart open, each time assured that God's steadfast love will welcome us with open arms.

God, you are the Holy Other. I want to love you with my whole self and be unafraid to admit that I sin. Let me pray with confidence but not with false pride in my status or accomplishments, and let me claim the promises you gave to Moses, the promise of redemption in You. Amen.

G ive me liberty, or give me death." That famous quotation of Patrick Henry comes to mind when I read this passage.

What a novel idea! Following God's precepts, laws, and instructions is actually a liberating action, not a limiting one. Most folks I know think of law as limit, not permission.

But the psalmist gets it. The psalmist knows that to walk in liberty means to follow the paths God lays before us. That way of walking means we put our whole self into the equation. We embody the promises and associated constraints of God's instructions. The promises are a strong shield that protects us from the taunts of those who find us different.

Without the freedom to live and love as God instructs, we might as well be dead. Give us liberty, indeed. I'll take salvation over death any day.

Great Teacher, I place my trust in your instructions and seek to walk in the ways you teach me. May my life be a living witness to the hope I place in you, and may others be led to walk in liberty and life. Amen.

*T*oday is Flag Day. This day commemorates the adoption of the flag of the United States, which happened by resolution of the Second Continental Congress in 1777.

The flag is an important symbol of our history and reminds us of the spirit of freedom that shaped our country. But that's all it is—a symbol. It should not be worshiped.

As this reading reminds us, "Where the Spirit of the Lord is, there is freedom" (v. 17). We should put aside anything that might veil our understanding of true freedom, including the secular symbol of the flag of the United States. Our freedom, as Christ followers, is situated in the eternal wisdom and promise of our triune God, whom we know as Father, Son, and Holy Spirit; Creator, Redeemer, and Sustainer.

It's hard to separate faith in God from love of country. If we understand our country to be of God, we ought to act accordingly and find ways to truly seek liberty and justice for all.

Give us the hope to act with boldness, fueled by the spirit and freedom we find in you, Jesus. Amen.

*O*h, Paul, you and your stumbling blocks. This time it's food, which is enough of a stumbling block for many. Too much, too little, not the right kind or quantity. What's a Christian to do?

We are to love one another. We are free to love, as Christ loved us. We are free to eat and drink and share our physical food and our spiritual food.

Some people need special diets to help them grow in faith. We need to set a good example and not erect barriers that could be avoided. It's like offering vegetarians veggie burgers cooked on a grill with chicken. Just because we don't mind doesn't mean it won't offend our friends.

What does Paul want us to know? He reminds us that we serve as examples; while we enjoy freedom in Christ, this freedom does not give us liberty to trample over others in our certainty of belief or strength of faith. By watching what we eat, we can lead others to improve and strengthen their diets.

God is great. God is good. Let us thank God for our food. By God's hand we all are fed. Thank you, God, for daily bread. Amen.

Be not hearers who forget what they hear, but doers who act. This is James's formula for perfect liberty. Perfectly simple, it's not.

To make the formula work, we do well to remember that the doctrines, theologies, beliefs, and practices that order faith mirror who we are. We may not even recognize ourselves if our beliefs lead us to embody self-serving, feel-good, inwardly focused ways of living. We need to see evidence of a true and lively faith.

What should we hope to see? Among other things, we are to minister to widows and orphans and try to live free of stain. While it is hard to imagine what it's like to remain unstained by the world, we know that God's Word is a perfect stain remover that can keep sin from holding us prisoner to our selfish desires. It is the kind of perfect liberty James is talking about.

Triune God, we look in a mirror and see ourselves, made in your image. Help us to be perfect, as you are perfect, as we learn to live within the liberating freedom of your perfect law of love. Amen.

*U*ubilee!" The shout rings out on Mobile Bay when nature mysteriously drives seafood onto the shore. Folks scramble to grab whatever the bay spits out. The catch is plentiful, unpredictable, and short-lived. No telling when it will happen again.

Not so the trumpet sound announcing the jubilee that happened every fifty years in Israel. It was a time of freedom from work and toil, a time of reuniting with family and friends. Jubilee was a time to shelter those who needed support and to redeem property on behalf of kinfolk who had fallen on hard times. It was an entire year of being free from producing goods, food, and work; a year of living off what the land provides; a time to love God freely and to celebrate the gifts graciously bestowed on all creation.

What would a jubilee year look like, feel like, be like, for you?

God of abundance, thank you for the blessings you unexpectedly provide. What a gift it would be to stop producing and live supportively, sharing the fruit of the land with all as they have need. May it be so, provider God; may it be so. Amen.

*T*his is one of my favorite passages in the Psalms. I love its assurances of God's steadfast love and exuberant thanksgivings for God's wonderful works of creation.

Perhaps you have a case of the "Mondays" today. This psalm is just about guaranteed to refresh your perspective on the day at hand and the future as God would have you encounter it.

To get a sense of this psalm, it is best said aloud. Go on, you can do it. Read each line, with gusto. Say it like you mean it, like you really believe in God's goodness, God's all-encompassing power to love us and provide for us.

Now, how do you feel? While saying this passage aloud won't solve the problems of your world this day, it should give you a sense of God's love and care. The God of gods and Lord of lords is One, Alone. And God loves you.

Thank you, loving God, for this reminder of your care for me and for all your good creation this day. With grateful thanks for your everlasting provision in my heart, may I go and share my gratitude with others. Amen.

*M*uch of our Christian journey deals with matters of covenant—God's covenant with humankind, for example, or the promises that we make to one another at the time of baptism, marriage, or ordination to a church office. In this passage from Paul's letter to the Romans, we run into expressions of covenant life once again. Circumcision as Paul refers to it here is a symbol of obedience to God's covenant.

Just as a sacrament may be understood as an outward sign of an inward grace, how we demonstrate our willingness to live according to God's law is an expression of God's grace to us. As Paul reminds us, it is not only a matter of outward appearances but a matter of the heart. If we put into practice what we hold dear in our hearts, our outward expressions of the grace of God we carry in our hearts is pleasing to God.

God, as I seek to walk with you, I pray that my faith is an outward expression of my commitment to love you with all my heart and to serve you with my whole self—body, mind, and spirit. Amen.

*T*oday we encounter Paul in full diatribe mode. He rails against those who explain away sinful human behavior by saying that God's righteousness and grace, freely given, fail to discourage it. For me it raises the question "How does my life reflect God's faithfulness and justice?"

People of faith, whether "cradle Christians" or those who come to the faith as older people, share the potential for sinful behavior and the same life-giving grace of God as given to us in Jesus Christ. God entrusts us to live as faithfully as we can while knowing that we will repeatedly fall short. We rely on God's faithfulness and justice to be there, regardless of our behavior, extending grace upon grace. It is very good news indeed. No matter how hard we try, we cannot nullify God's faithfulness and justice for us and for the entire world.

Gracious God, you entrust us to be stewards of teachings, to live like the good news matters to us. The gift of your grace is meant to encourage us to live this way. It is not meant to excuse sinful behavior. Forgive me when I take your faithfulness and justice for granted. Amen.

*A*s a child, my youngest son was likely to refer to nearly any meaningful act connected to a holiday as a "tradition." Traditions included using a particular electric knife to carve the turkey and the arrangement of candles on a birthday cake. His understanding of tradition helped him make sense of his world.

As Christians, we are called to be stewards of the traditions we have received from our elders. These traditions help us make sense of our world as we seek to understand and apply the early church's postresurrection values to our lives.

The two concluding verses in today's passage form a wishful prayer addressed to God. The prayer is for our continued comfort and hope and for strength as we seek to live faithfully. I don't know of a better prayer to pray today.

Now may our Lord Jesus Christ himself and God our Father, who loved us and through grace gave us eternal comfort and good hope, comfort your hearts and strengthen them in every good work and word. Amen.

*T*his is one of my touchstone passages in Scripture. A favorite anthem, "Offertory," by John Ness Beck, features its words. My mother inscribed this passage in the Bible I received on my ordination. My mother and I shared a love of all kinds of music, and I feel a deeper connection to her through the music I hear in this passage.

I look at her handwriting in my Bible and think about how she lived out the requirements outlined in this well-known text. I sing the words in verses 6–8, which outline the requirements of the Lord for those who follow him: to seek justice, love kindness, and walk humbly with our God. I wonder if my life mirrors these requirements, at least a little bit. I know my mother's did.

Someday, I hope my sons will read these verses and think of me, of my mother, and all the saints who seek to embody these requirements of the One who shows us the way.

Great Teacher, your lessons outline the paths you would have us take, the guidelines for lives faithfully lived in discipleship. You have indeed shown us what is good. May it always be so. Amen.

Yesterday's reflection focused on what the Lord requires of us as disciples: seeking justice, loving kindness, walking humbly with God. Today we are reminded that these requirements are God's ways—the ways of truth and justice.

In the midst of amazing visions of heavenly portents, angels, fire, and glassy seas, the voices of a choir singing songs of liberation, of Moses, and the Lamb break forth. The voices and visions witness to the amazing deeds and history of the Lord God Almighty.

Just and true are God's ways. As ruler of all the nations, of all people and countries, God is the One who receives our fear, our love, and our worship. Everything else pales in comparison with God's great deeds, God's true and just ways. We who would seek to follow those ways had best get practicing.

Amazing, gracious God, we cannot imagine the future without you. We cannot visualize what the day of your coming kingdom will look like when we see it. Great and amazing are your deeds; just and true are your ways. May we seek to follow in the paths you set before us. Amen.

This week begins where last week left off—continuing our reflection about God's justice and love. Our gratitude for these gifts should fuel our responses to them. To what should our gratitude lead?

The last verse in the passage sums it up: "Justice, and only justice, you shall pursue, so that you may live and occupy the land that the LORD your God is giving you" (16:20). The pursuit of justice includes caring for widows, orphans, and strangers, showing no partiality.

Imagine what the pursuit of justice would look like in your circumstances. What's going on? What does it sound like? Who else is in the picture? What's the lay of this blessed land that you occupy?

The pursuit of justice is difficult, as local and international news reminds us. But if we don't deliberately pursue it, we'll never find it. Get going. What's holding you back?

Guide my steps, God, as I step out in faith this day and each day, in pursuit of the love, justice, and peace you desire for your creation. May I walk in your way, loving and serving you with all my heart and soul. Amen.

These are uneasy words, these warnings from Ezekiel. They seem to be spoken in impatience and anger in response to the whining of the people of Israel. Once again, God's people are struggling to do as God requires and are not shy about expressing it.

God's judgment is not to be ignored if we wish to live fully. But the death threat in verse 26 is not the last word, fortunately. Assurances follow it—assurances that require us to turn away from sin and to God.

I find it more difficult to examine my transgressions than to see them in others. My heart and spirit are heavy with this realization. I do indeed wish to cast off this heaviness. It's much easier to move when I can be light on my feet and in my heart.

God's invitation to repent leads to a renewed heart and spirit. And who can resist such an invitation when it leads to a fair, full-of-life future?

God of love and justice, when I worry about what is fair, I turn away from your justice and righteousness. It's hard to turn around, to repent and start over, when burdened by sin. Help me turn to you, God, in pursuit of your everlasting life. Amen.

*H*annah is one strong petitioner, isn't she? Pouring out her troubles to God from the depth of her soul, her earnest faith catches Eli's eye and God's ear. Her earnest petition is granted. Sadness leaves her as her son is born—a tangible response to prayer if I've ever seen one!

I wish it were so easy. I know many women who pray and pray for a child, who must be as earnest a group of petitioners as Hannah ever was. Yet their wombs and arms remain empty. Sadness floods their eyes and hearts.

Perhaps you are one of these women. If you are, accept my earnest prayer for you to know God's peace.

Perhaps you know of such a woman. If so, offer an earnest prayer for her and her family that they hear God's loving response and that sadness vanishes from their faces and hearts.

Lord, hear our prayers on behalf of others, especially those women who long for a child as Hannah did. Today we pray to you on their behalf. Fill them with peace even as they continue to wait and pray. Amen.

*H*annah's gift from the Lord turned out to be her gift to the Lord. She returned to the temple to see Samuel fulfill his duties to Eli earnestly and honestly. But his colleagues, Eli's sons, were scoundrels. They turned sacrificial gifts into the spoils of their office. The Lord saw through their deceit and dishonest service. No rewards were coming their way, that's for sure.

This passage seems to say that God rewards the righteous and punishes the wicked. Elsewhere in Scripture we encounter views that challenge the premise that all who suffer are being punished. And as we noted yesterday, we know of good people who suffer—of women who remain childless after their earnest petitions, for example.

Like me, you may be quick to count your blessings. But stop and think about it—what have you given to the Lord that would come close to matching Hannah's gift?

Perhaps we need to focus on what we are willing to give to God before we earnestly pray for God's good gift. Our brokenness may lead to surprising gifts before we expect something in return.

Generous God, receive our gifts of self and service. Show us how our gifts from you and our gifts to you might be one and the same. Amen.

I'm reminded of this passage when I sing this line from a familiar hymn: "I have heard you calling in the night." I heard my children call out to me when they were little; members of a confirmation class on a retreat have kept me awake more than once.

But God's voice? How do I really *know* God's voice at any hour of the day or night? And how might I respond if I received such a chilling and challenging message such as the one Samuel received from God?

God's call is usually two-sided, I've found. There's great joy along the way and great blessings. But there's a price, too. Heeding God's call can be risky and rewarding. Scary and surprising. If we speak up in response to God's call, we might be the recipient of a message that will change our lives and the lives of others.

Ever-living, ever-calling God, open my heart and ears to your voice, day or night. Prepare me to hear your message in your good time. Prepare me to receive the news, to be blessed by it, and to respond faithfully. Amen.

This passage reminds me of Proverbs 3:5 with its reminders to trust in the Lord with all our hearts, to rely on God's ways, and to trust the path God has set before us.

That's what I see happening here. Samuel became a trustworthy prophet because he listened to God and to those God sent along the way to guide him. Yes, his ears got stopped up occasionally, as his later escapades clearly illustrate. His ears stop up when he listens to himself or other human beings. When he trusts God, God entrusts him to bring the word to the world.

So I wonder how my word—words like these on this page— will be received by you. Will they honor God's message? Will they reflect my trust in seeking God's way, instead of my way? I can only hope and pray that it will be so.

God, you invite us to trust fully in you. Help us let go of our fears and foolishness so that we may step out in faith by our living. Help us to be trustworthy stewards of your teachings as we share them with others. Amen.

*H*oly, holy, holy, Lord God Almighty!" I hear the strains of that marvelous hymn echo in this reading. The psalmist reminds us of other revered servant-leaders—Moses, Aaron, and Samuel. And then the psalmist reminds us of something that we might rather forget.

We are reminded that the Lord avenged the wrongdoings of these revered prophets and was forgiving to them. It doesn't say the Lord looked the other way and let them off the hook. A price was paid; suffering and brokenness occurred. And God was faithful—loving—forgiving, still.

The twenty-first-century Samanthas and Samuels that will arise as God's revered prophets should take heart in the assurance this text offers. In our frailty and sinfulness, we can claim God's justice and God's love.

Holy God, One in Three—Creator, Christ, and Spirit—let us always exalt you above all, even as we listen for you speaking to us. Amen.

*H*ave you served on a jury, judged a competition, or served as a soccer referee? It's hard work, sorting through testimony or attending to the rules. It's hard work attending to all the people who are involved.

Samuel proved more than capable of serving as judge for the people of Israel. As he rode circuit, he performed his priestly duties consistently, kindly, and fairly. Enemies were restrained. The justice he meted out was more legal than military justice compared to that of his predecessors. His righteous judgment encouraged repentance among God's people; God responded favorably.

There are things that distract us from following God with all our hearts. And there are times we catch ourselves judging other faithful people on the basis of how well we think they live out their faith. May we be as faithful a judge as Samuel and as true in our repentance and encouragement of others.

God of justice and mercy, help us resist idols and our tendency to see signs of sin in others before we see our own. Teach us repentance and faithfulness; let us leave the judging to you. Amen.

*H*ow good are you at asking directions? Do you wait until you're completely turned around, or do you rely on your GPS or road map when you head into unfamiliar territory? Do you rely on someone to show you the way?

David, no longer a shepherd boy, uses a divine GPS to direct his journey. He asks, and the Lord sends him to establish a settlement. He continues to explore the complexity of maintaining faithful relationships with God and among God's people. In this passage, loyalty to a departed leader (Saul) results in God's blessing.

In our contentious political climate, people located all along the theological or political continuum rarely find common ground and unity. Opponents are quick to claim God's favor and blessing for their positions. I don't know about you, but these days I sometimes wish inquiring of the Lord in matters of faith and politics could be as simple as it was for David.

Gracious God, lead us where you want us to go. Open our ears to hear you clearly. Teach us to place our trust in you. Amen.

*W*hat an affirmation of God's strength and protection is this poetic summary of David's life, his walk with God. Read the entire chapter for the rest of the story.

When I read verses 19–20 I am reminded of how God stuck with David in the midst of his calamities—calamities that were of his making. Think of Uriah and Bathsheba. Think of Absalom. David's behaviors at times were far from delightful. Yet the text attests to God's deliverance in spite of the occasions of blatant disregard of God's laws. To God indeed goes the glory for David's deliverance from all his enemies—including himself.

This gives me hope. I'm not perfect—more like David than I'd like to believe. I don't expect the earth to rock and roll as a sign of God's deliverance. A sense of peace would be sufficient to know God accepts me just as I am. It worked for David. May it be so for everyone who calls upon God for deliverance.

We rejoice in the promise of your deliverance, great God of creation. Take us as we are; free us from the sin that separates us from you. Bind our hearts to yours forever. Amen.

*T*oday is Independence Day, when we revel in all things patriotic. We remember those who serve in the military and honor those who have served, who have emerged from service wounded, and who have lost their lives.

In light of this passage, which highlights God's guidance, we do well to remember that God is God of all creation. God is a shield and refuge for all. In the past as in the present, God followers of different faiths face one another in armed conflict. Moreover, other passages of Scripture tell us that God shows no partiality.

I am the mother of two sons who serve in the United States Army. As you read this, one of them will be in Afghanistan, halfway through his tour. I pray for God to bless and keep him and his troop safe. I also pray that God will protect all men and women in uniform in service of all countries. Yes, that means I pray for those whom my sons face as enemies. I hope you will join me, because as Christians that is what we are called to do.

Protector God, keep all who serve our country in your tender care. Keep them safe, and guide them safely home. Share your protection generously with all your children. Amen.

I find myself humming the spiritual that asks God to "guide my feet while I run this race." I'm struck by images of God as our rock of ages. With God's help, we can be sure-footed people, walking confidently ahead into whatever comes our way.

Nevertheless, I stumble. I lose my way. My hands weaken. I lose confidence and feel far from secure. I know that God is my firm foundation; God will lead me into the future, whatever it holds. What I don't know for certain is that last part—"whatever it holds."

I think of David and how he faithfully, albeit imperfectly, continued to follow God through times of grief and shame as well as victory and celebration. He didn't know what his future held either. With this reminder, I feel a bit more secure. That shield of salvation is what I most need to put before me. With that, I have all I need.

Mighty God, give us sureness of purpose, a clear path, and steadfast resolve to follow you wherever you lead. Guide our feet, Lord, every step of the way. Amen.

*T*he phrase *steadfast love* appears at least 121 times in the NRSV translation of the Old Testament. The word *steadfast* occurs close to 600 times. The premise of God's steadfast love undergirds much of the entire canon of Scripture, both Old and New Testaments. For many of us, those two words are the foundation of our faith.

It is fitting to praise God at all times and in all things. Scripture teaches that our motivation to serve God is gratitude for God's steadfast love through the grace of our Lord Jesus Christ, God's love, and the companionship of the Holy Spirit.

As you read, think of a favorite hymn of praise. Now lift your voice in exultant praise of our God. Sing with energy—as if you mean it—and let that energy fuel you for the work and witness you are called to do. In all you do, remember that it is the steadfast love of God that upholds you. Praise God, from whom all blessings flow!

We will sing of your steadfast love forever, O God. You are the rock of our salvation in all generations. Amen.

But those who are noble plan noble things, and by noble things they stand" (v. 8). *Noble* isn't a word that most of us encounter, or even use, very often. That's sort of sad, I think. Something—or someone—noble is of an exalted moral character, admirable, dignified in expression, impressive, or magnificent.

Perhaps we have grown to expect mediocrity these days, in spite of aspiring to excellence or at least to being above average. God inspires us to nobility of purpose, to an admirable way of living before others and before God.

Our God reigns in and over all creation. God's creation is magnificent. It is impressive. It is noble. As part of creation, perhaps we can claim some of that nobility for ourselves and plan accordingly. God stands by us, and we stand by God.

Eternal God, you continue to rule over creation. Inspire us— your princes and princesses—to a noble way of living and being. As stewards of your good creation, may we seek justice and peace. Amen.

*D*awn breaks on a new day, shedding light on what the night had hidden. It slips into our darkened rooms through the slits in the blinds and greets us persistently, welcomed or not.

So it is with justice and equity. As surely as the dawn illuminates our bedrooms each morning, God's will shines amid the darkness and evil of our hearts. Just as the new day will triumph over the passing night, so too will God's justice and equity bring the world to peace.

God expects—commands—human beings to love one another fairly. Too many of us are not gentle. We are oftentimes harsh, like thorns in the flesh of the powerless and the oppressed. Yet the Son will forever rise, lighting the horizon—indeed, illuminating all things!

God, help me this day to lead with justice and equity. Let my life shine with your light, today and always. Amen.

*M*ost people agree that there is a difference between being wise and being smart, between having wisdom and having knowledge. While it's hard to put into words, a wise person exhibits depth and maturity that are not always apparent in a smart person.

For Paul, wisdom comes with an enlightened vision from the heart that illumines a purpose, a goal, and a faith in God's immeasurable greatness. Regardless of where we find ourselves in the world's economy—as teacher, businessperson, health care professional, at-home parent, retired, or unemployed—we seek God's calling on our lives. We pursue the goals that arise from our calling in all that we do, trusting in God's greatness, shown to us in the life, death, and resurrection of Christ along the way.

May it be so, this day and always!

God, grant us wisdom to seek your purpose for our lives. As we live into your calling, help us remember to place our trust not in things of this world but in you and you alone. Amen.

Safety and prosperity do not always come to "the faithful ones," do they? Despite the words of wisdom that come from the mouths of the faithful, troubles befall them. Though God's law is in the hearts of the faithful and the steps of the righteous seem sure, the wicked prevail. Here, in the time between Good Friday and Easter Sunday, we don't always see God's work clearly. We are a broken and fearful people in a broken and fearful world. We are called to goodness and faithfulness, but we are also told to wait. To wait for the Lord. To wait and follow God's way in the meantime. God will not forsake.

It is hard when God's time is not our time. But in faithfulness, we are reminded to be patient. God is faithful; God will neither abandon nor forsake us. This is great news!

God of all that is good, keep us faithful. Give us patience to wait for you, trusting that we will not be forsaken. Amen.

*W*hat does it mean to be loved? Does being God's beloved mean that no harm will befall us? By no means! David's name means "Beloved." Despite the fact that David's sin was great, he was still God's beloved. No, God did not remove the consequences for David's sin, but God's compassion allowed David and Bathsheba to bear another son, whom they named Solomon.

We, too, are God's beloved. God is loving and just with us. No, we are not always rescued from the consequences of our missteps, but we do trust that God can and does make good things come out of the valleys of darkness in our lives.

You are a beloved child of God. Never forget your belovedness.

God, thank you for calling us beloved. Help us live more and more like your beloved people each day, sharing your love and your faithfulness with all those whom we meet. Amen.

*E*very four years, Americans have the privilege of electing a president. Each January following a presidential election we celebrate with pomp and circumstance a presidential inauguration. It is indeed a lavish affair, with balls and dinners and parties galore.

A four-year term pales in comparison to the reigns of kings in the Old Testament. Imagine what it was like for Solomon to be anointed king after David's long and successful reign of forty years!

The transfer of power of any kind is a momentous occasion. Likewise, the privilege of power comes with momentous responsibility. Despite the amount of power we may wield in our day-to-day lives, it is important to acknowledge that all power ultimately lies with God. When we are in tune with God, our power can be used to accomplish God's work in the world. Just as God used the reigns of both David and Solomon, so too can God use even us!

Remind us today and always, O God, that you are ruler of all. Keep us humble and faithful as we bow to your rule and to your power. Amen.

*A*donijah's plan was to succeed his father, David, as king. However, God had other plans. When the plans were made clear and Solomon was anointed king, Adonijah and Solomon showed each other grace. Adonijah bowed in humility and accepted God's plan. Solomon showed compassion on his former rival and sent him home unharmed.

In today's world, competition spans all ages and demographics: from our statehouses to our places of business, from our classrooms to our playing fields. What if those in power today were more like Adonijah and Solomon, modeling forgiveness and graciousness rather than aggression and rivalry? What might our lives look like if graciousness and cooperation were more evident in our day-to-day interactions than hostility and competition?

Grant us this day, O God, kind and generous hearts. Help us to strive for cooperation over competition, for grace over rudeness, for peace over strife. Amen.

 S olomon is often equated with wisdom. God bestowed wisdom upon Solomon that surpassed even the wisest of his day. He had wisdom to heed God's instruction and to set goals with it in mind. He had discernment to follow God's instructions and God's alone. Solomon had understanding that allowed him to be well loved and respected by those whom he ruled.

Solomon's wisdom was as vast as the sand on the seashore while he ruled the descendants of Abraham that were as numerous as the stars in the sky. Neither the sand nor the stars can be counted. Both are vast and overwhelming in number, just as God's faithfulness is vast and overwhelming.

In his wisdom, Solomon recognized the power and amazing faithfulness of God. If we are wise, we too will seek and heed God's call, trusting that the love of God is boundless and the promises of God are steadfast.

Grant, O Lord, that on this day we might be gifted with the wisdom of Solomon and the courage to take the steps that you desire us to take. Amen.

*T*hese women have put Solomon in a very difficult position! However, with seeming ease, he is able to take the circumstance at hand and, in his wisdom, use it to affect justice in the midst of their dispute. The true mother of the living child was made clear to everyone because of Solomon's wise solution.

Wisdom without practice is hollow. Think back to a time in your life when you faced a problem. The internal struggle at such a time can be difficult—even painful. By being open to God's light, we can learn a way forward through prayer and discernment. Even when we have a path ahead, further action is necessary to take the steps down that path. Because Solomon put his wisdom into practice during his reign, God was able to use him to execute justice and righteousness. When we put our wisdom into practice through prayer, discernment, and action, God can do amazing things through us as well!

Help me to be wise today, God. Help me to seek you, to listen to you, and to respond to your leading this day and always. Amen.

*H*ave you ever made a bad decision? The younger son finds himself making a bad decision soon after he receives the inheritance he requested. It is often too easy for us to judge him for his poor choices. However, we are not so different from the prodigal son. We ask God to bless us, and then we squander those blessings on our version of dissolute living. We do our thing; we make our decisions. We forget to follow God, who leads us.

Like the prodigal son, we occasionally make bad decisions. And like the jubilant father, God welcomes us with open arms and joyous compassion when we return. Despite the fact that we have sinned and are not worthy to be called children of God, our return is cause for God's celebration, indeed the celebration of the entire household of God. God's grace is sufficient. God's love never fails.

Thank you, good and gracious God, for your boundless forgiveness found in Christ Jesus and for your unending love for all of creation. Keep us close to you always. Remind us to seek your will in all that we do. Amen.

*S*in is a very real part of who we are. There are signs of oppression all around us. Despite the evils of the world, the psalmist reminds us that God's enemies will be scattered and driven away. The God whom we worship will one day rise up and defeat the principalities and powers of this world. It is an assurance to which we can cling during our darkest, hardest times.

But what about today? Where is God when the principalities and powers seem to be winning now? The truth is that the God we worship does rise up, even today. The oppressed and powerless are protected and defended by God just as they were ages ago. When it seems that evil is getting the upper hand, we should be joyful before God. Sing praises and lift up the Lord's name, trusting that God will provide a home in which his children will live and will lead them to true freedom and prosperity.

We praise your name, O God, for the ways that you are at work in this world. Help us remember that even on our darkest days, you are with us, rising up to scatter the enemy. Amen.

*W*hen I was a child, this story from Luke confused me. The story is often called the tale of the widow's mite, and as a young child, I thought it was about the widow's *might*, the widow's strength. When I finally realized that the widow in the story was merely a poor, insignificant woman, I wondered what was so mighty about her. Of course, the cause of my confusion was an error in homonyms, and I ultimately began to hear the story the correct way.

Recently, however, I have come to prefer my childhood understanding of the story. Perhaps the widow did give a mite, but in so doing, she showed great might. The mighty demand and often receive respect and priority. They greedily climb up the backs of others simply to gain higher stature, and then give insignificant portions back to God for all to see their "generosity." They have much and give little. But this woman, this widow, had little and gave much. By giving all that she had, she showed great might, great strength.

God, you have given us gifts beyond measure. May we be mighty like the widow, giving generously out of gratitude rather than selfishly for show. Amen.

The Bible is filled with stories of hospitality. It was not uncommon for weary travelers to find refuge in the homes of strangers. It would be wonderful if we could share such hospitality today, but unfortunately, the world is different now. It would be far too dangerous to welcome total strangers into our homes. However, we can show hospitality in a variety of other ways.

We can invite the widower that we see occasionally at the grocery store for a cup of coffee at a nearby coffee shop. Perhaps we can cook and serve a meal at a homeless shelter on a cold winter night. Offering to host a toddler in your home for a few hours while his parents enjoy time alone is another form of hospitality. When we open ourselves to friends or strangers in these ways, we invite God to work in our lives in new and different ways. How can you show hospitality today?

Thank you, God, for the ways that you work in and through us in our daily lives. Open our eyes this day to opportunities for hospitality. Amen.

*T*he sharing of hospitality creates a unique relationship between people. When we show hospitality out of our love for God rather than our desire to be repaid in kind, we often find ourselves in relationships that are mutually interdependent and equally beneficial. So it is with the Shunammite woman and the prophet Elisha. Their dance of giving and receiving has bonded them in such a way that she is able to approach him boldly at a time of great need, and he is able to respond.

The passage reminds us that the dance of hospitality creates relationships that go beyond one simple act of hospitality and the gracious repayment of that kindness. Can you think of a time when an act of hospitality led to a new relationship in your life—a relationship that has created space for God's work to be done? If so, take a moment and give thanks to God for the beauty of the hospitality dance in your life this day.

Thank you, God, for the gift of hospitality. Enable me today and always to give and receive it graciously, creating more space for your work in this world. Amen.

The death of a child defies the natural order of life, and the pain that comes in the wake of such a loss is unimaginable. Resurrection stories are rare these days, but they were more frequent in the days of Elisha. Because of this, the mother is determined not just to sit by and passively accept her son's death. She is single-minded in her drive to find Elisha and insistent that Elisha see to the son. Their dance of hospitality has freed her to seek him in her time of great need. With care and tending, their relationship has grown into one on which she can rely for support. Because she is able to go to Elisha with her need, God restores life to her son.

Few relationships simply happen without effort. However, with time and attention, they can add beauty and strength to our lives. How do we build relationships of support with one another today? How is God at work in those relationships?

Gracious God, thank you for the ways that you weave us together as your family. May we continue to nurture and grow in our relationships with those around us, today and always. Amen.

$\mathcal{J}$ust when we thought we'd seen the last of the Shunammite woman, she appears again. The deep trust she places in Elisha is not surprising now, given their ongoing relationship. When he instructs her to "go with your household" and leave for seven years, she does. No deals are made; no what-ifs are asked. This is trust, plain and simple.

How difficult is it for us to trust God fully? Even when the cards are stacked against us, as they seemed to be for this Shunammite woman, are we able to step out in faith, fully trusting in God's care, in God's providence? The Shunammite woman was willing to open herself up to a relationship with Elisha many years before. God works in her life through this relationship in amazing ways. Imagine what God can do through us when we open ourselves to hospitality and the relationships it often brings.

Thank you, God, for the way you work through those in our lives like Elisha to accomplish your will. Help us always to be open to others, realizing that by opening ourselves to others, we are opening ourselves to you. Amen.

Reminders are helpful. Parents remind their children of multiple things every day. Electronic devices remind the workforce of appointments, meetings, and deadlines with relentless beeps and chirps. Kitchen devices beep to remind us that dinner is ready or the coffee is brewed. Even the sound of the garbage truck rumbling down the street serves as a reminder to roll the can to the curb.

In a world where we are often judged from countless sides, today's passage serves as a comforting reminder that God alone is our ultimate judge. While we may not always live up to the standards of our family members, our employers, our parishioners, or our loved ones, God alone is our judge, our ruler, and our king. God alone will save us. May we be ready to stand before God at the appointed time and hear God say, "Well done, good and faithful servant!"

God of all, we acknowledge your might and majesty this day. Ready our hearts and our minds to meet you at the place of broad rivers and streams with the sure and certain knowledge that you alone are our judge. Amen.

*I*t seems that every fall we are bombarded by mean-spirited, vitriolic political ads and propaganda. No election season is ever easy or fun; some in recent memory seem particularly unpleasant. Perhaps it's due to our weariness with being in an "economic downturn" for over three years or a growing dissatisfaction with the state of our country, combined with impatience over slow progress to get us back on track. Regardless of whom or what we blame, most of us are totally exasperated by the time election season rolls around.

Imagine for a moment what it might be like if we were to pray for our elected leaders, regardless of party or platform, using the words found in today's passage. Do we truly believe that God can, will, and does use all manner of people, despite their political affiliation, to accomplish God's good purpose? If so, then praying for our leaders might be the best thing we could do for our seemingly broken system.

Reread the passage again, praying earnestly for all elected officials. Amen.

*P*salm 119 contains beautiful meditations on God's law; these eight verses offer a wonderful prelude to the longest of the psalms. Take a moment to reread these verses, pondering these questions as you read:

On a scale of 1 to 10, how happy are you with your life?

Do you keep God's decrees?

Do you seek God with your whole heart and walk in God's ways?

Do you do no wrong?

Individual responses to the first question will vary, but answers to the next ones will likely resemble these: "Heavens, no!" Or possibly, "I do my best but fail miserably on many days." Or even a sarcastic, "Yeah, right!"

While we are called to strive every day to be more like Jesus, the law no longer binds us. Christ frees us from it. This freedom does not come cheap, certainly not for Christ and not for us either. We are called, though, to offer our gratitude and our very selves to God in return. May it be so!

God, help us be more like you. On days when we fail, remind us that you love us still. Amen.

*W*hat is at your life's center? What is it that motivates, inspires, and challenges you? What is it that keeps you going each day, each week, each month?

Well-known organizational consultant Stephen Covey has said, "Whatever is at the center of our life will be the source of our security, guidance, wisdom, and power." If we believe him and if we were honest with our responses to the above questions, what does that say about us? What can we do about it?

Job has not had the easiest time of things. In fact, Job is probably the epitome of undeserved suffering. Yet in the midst of his story, we find this treatise about wisdom and understanding, reminding Job of what he already knows. True wisdom is the fear of God, and true understanding is evidenced by departure from evil.

How might our lives be different if we lived with a fearful respect for God and with a true desire to turn from all that is evil?

Grant us, O Lord, the strength to resist evil. Keep us ever mindful of your authority and your power, today and always. Amen.

*H*ave you ever had one of those days? You know, one of those days when you longed to stay in bed. When you finally got up, your day included two missed appointments, a key locked inside the car, spilt morning coffee, and a burnt chicken dinner.

Days like that make us feel powerless. Days like that make us feel helpless. Perhaps that is how Jehoshaphat felt as he stood in God's house, saying, "Are you not God? Do you not rule, God? We are lost, helpless, and powerless. We are relying solely on you, God!"

Sure enough, God responds: "Do not fear, . . . for the battle is not yours but God's" (v. 15).

A dinner out, followed by a nice long soak in the tub may help a bad day in the short run. In the end, remember God's words to Jehoshaphat and his people: "Do not fear, my child. The battle is not yours but God's." We stake our life on the belief that the battle, indeed the war, has already been won. Thanks be to God!

God, remind me on difficult days that not only the battle but also the war has been won, through the life, death, and resurrection of your son, Jesus Christ. Amen.

*F*or centuries, hide-and-seek has been a favorite children's game. A newer version of the old classic is called "Sardines," which is essentially hide-and-seek in reverse.

Another popular game is a scavenger hunt. The older version consists of giving each team a list of difficult-to-find items. The newer version takes advantage of digital technology, requiring the players to capture images of specific items.

What is it about hide-and-seek games that make them fun for all ages? Imagine if we all found seeking God as alluring as seeking a hidden person, a green paper clip, or a picture of two people in front of a "No Trespassing" sign.

Jehoshaphat sought God; he walked in the ways of God's commandments. Imagine what the world might look like if we were to seek God with the same excitement and perseverance we display when seeking the one hiding or the elusive green paper clip!

God, give us the passion to seek you first in all that we do. Give us courage to walk in your ways this day and forevermore. Amen.

A recent incident in my life involved our newly licensed fifteen-year-old driver, the rear end of an automobile owned by a kind and gracious older woman, a county police officer, and a stern yet fair judge.

Our son was cited for following too closely. As a new driver, he did not have the experience to react quickly enough to stop our large, heavy automobile. The other party did not want him to receive a citation, but the officer had no choice. She encouraged us to contest it in court. We did and encountered a compassionate, caring judge, who epitomized the Chronicler's admonition to judge on behalf of the Lord, not on behalf of human beings.

My son learned a valuable lesson that day. He learned about driving, yes, but he also learned about humility, about admitting one's mistakes honestly. He learned about compassion. He learned about grace.

When I look back on it now, I daresay that he learned a bit about God.

God of grace, we thank you for your love and forgiveness. As we go about our lives, may we look with your kindness upon those we encounter each day. Amen.

*T*oday's world cries out for justice with every breath. The pain of individuals creates a spirit of oppression and anger. The pain of a group of people creates a spirit of hatred and violence. The pain of a country creates suspicion and warfare. Sadly, it seems that all we can do is sit and wait. In the midst of our pain-filled world, Malachi's words strike a chord: "Have we not all one Father? Has not one God created us? Why then are we faithless to one another?" (v. 10).

As the prophet reminds us, God desires godly offspring. God desires us to be faithful to God and to one another. The God of justice is not absent but present, crying with us over injustice in our world. Though we may feel abandoned at times, as if God has forsaken us, this is not the case. Where is the God of justice? The God of justice is among us even now; God calls us back to a better way, back to God's way.

May we heed the call.

God of justice, make us more faithful. Help us to see you even on the darkest of days. Surround us all with your care, and guide us home. Amen.

*I*magine what it is like to be in a dark room without a slice of light. I imagine that is what it is like to be so deeply entrenched in injustice that the shining light of God's justice is not visible. History is full of dark days when all hope seemed lost. God's story as found in the Bible is a reflection of that history, part of humanity's story as told by God and God's people.

Now visualize a tiny bit of light finding its way into the dark room. Hope is restored! So it is with God's justice. Our darkest days seem utterly hopeless, with justice elusive, seemingly never to be found. Then we lift our eyes to heaven just as Nebuchadnezzar did, and our reason returns to us. We give praise and honor to God Most High. We declare with the great king that yes, indeed, God's works are truth and God's ways are justice!

God of justice, help us to be a part of that light shining in the world's darkness, this day and always. Amen.

*I*f God wandered among today's churches, cities, and towns, what would God think? What would God think about our worship, our life together as the body of Christ, or our daily prayers? What would God think while wandering our marketplaces or our halls of government?

God was not pleased during the time of Isaiah's writing, having grown impatient and intolerant of the people's behavior. Their immoral ways and hollow religious practices had become abhorrent.

God is likely not pleased with us today. God's response to Judah in this passage speaks just as clearly to us. "You self-serving hypocrites!" God replies, then proceeds to make it very clear what is desired—a fast far more difficult than the ritualistic ones they have been observing, yet a fast far more worthwhile. Fight injustice. Free the prisoners. Share with one another. Shelter and clothe the homeless.

How are we doing with God's desired fast? What fasts of our making can we give up in order to fast as God desires?

Gracious God, help us to reach out to others. Remind us each day that you desire true community for us, and help us live into that desire. Amen.

*F*ool me once, shame on you. Fool me twice, shame on me."
When one's trust is broken, it is hard to regain. God's people
have once again disappointed God, broken God's trust. Anytime
this happens, it is helpful for the one who breaks the trust
to know what steps must be taken in order to restore it. The
relationship of trust begins anew, with God promising again
to be faithful.

The God we worship is a faithful and covenantal God—a God
who promises to guide us continually along the way. However,
over time, God learned that we would fail. Therefore, God
came down in the flesh to show us the way and to save us from
our hopelessness. In that way, God sent a light to rise in the
darkness. God rebuilt the ancient ruins and has repaired the
breach in our relationship with him. Thanks be to God!

*Thank you, God, for the continual guidance that you provide
for us. Thank you too for joining us in our earthly walk to make
right the things that we never can. Amen.*

*P*rayer changes things." We've seen those words on bumper stickers, greeting cards, and coffee mugs. We believe them, don't we? Otherwise, why would we pray at all? Prayer makes a difference!

Our world is rife with injustice. For centuries, faithful Christians have been praying for justice to rain down like waters, yet justice is still not a reality for all people. Does that mean that our prayers are not working? Certainly not! We've been waiting for centuries—between that dark Friday and the glorious resurrection Sunday. Therefore, we pray with persistence and patience. Justice will come in God's good time. In the meantime, we cry to God day and night, trusting that God's timing is perfect and God's faithfulness is assured.

Not all bumper-sticker theology rings true. However, this particular catchphrase reflects a certainty. Trust in the power of prayer. Trust in the One God to whom we pray through Jesus Christ by the power of the Holy Spirit.

God, thank you for being at work in our lives and through our prayers. Help us to trust that all will be well in your good and perfect time. Amen.

*M*uch like Dr. Seuss's character Yertle the Turtle, those in power during Amos's day climbed on the backs of others in order to ascend higher and higher. Amos reveals God's plan for the Yertles of his time. There will come a day when those in power will not enjoy the benefits of their harvest. The time is coming, but in the meantime, God calls us to a different way.

How can we love the good and establish justice? Begin with those with whom you are closest. Have patience with your children; show kindness toward your spouse and gentleness toward friends. Outside the home, support charities. Advocate for those who have no voice. Fight for those whose rights have been denied. It matters not how we work on God's behalf to fulfill the coming kingdom. It simply matters that we do it—for ourselves and for those to come.

God, we thank you for loving us and for giving us the freedoms that we have. Help us to use our gifts and skills to love the good and establish justice, for the sake of your coming kingdom. Amen.

The psalmist reminds us to keep our focus on God. Praise God, and place your trust in God rather than in the powers of this earth.

The powers of the earth are passing; they are transient and not worthy of our trust. One administration leads to another; a boss is transferred or resigns; the economy is unreliable; and we find no real security in human institutions.

Those who entrust their lives to God can see evidence of God's presence in their lives: they are fed; they are set free; their eyes are opened to the truth of God's benevolence.

When we live a life of faith, it is the truth. We may live a simple life, one of service to others, one focused on hearth and home and time in prayer. This simple life is its own reward. When we open our hearts to God, good things flow.

O God of assurance, help me to put my trust in you. I will praise you, steadfast God, and sing your praises all of my life. Amen.

The storms and hail have destroyed the early crop of flax and barley in Egypt. Pharaoh summons Moses and asks that the destruction be stopped. Moses agrees even though he knows Pharaoh is not conceding to God, only to the power of the storms.

Moses goes out of the city and raises his hands to God, and the storms cease. Just as Moses thought, Pharaoh's heart is hard; he does not allow the Israelites to go.

Moses suspected that the promise of Pharaoh was hollow. Yet rather than try to reason, convince, or control Pharaoh, Moses took him at his word and let the consequences come as they would.

Moses' faith was in God, not in some hollow promise of an Egyptian king. Moses acted in faith, stopped the plague of hailstorms, and waited for Pharaoh. God proved to be faithful and true to the people of Israel.

O God of Moses and Aaron, you are faithful and just, true to your promise to deliver. May I place my trust in you rather than the powers of the world. Amen.

*D*oes this passage mean that we are to practice discrimination? The language here is harsh and unforgiving, so different from the God of grace and mercy that we know.

Ezra was written when the Hebrew people were establishing their community following the exile in Babylon. They sought to build stability as a people and a nation in conformity with the law of God. As part of this effort, concerns that land and wealth remain with the people of Israel led to a ban on intermarriage, which prevented the riches of Israel from being inherited by foreigners.

Political and economic stability were important for the rebuilding efforts. It may sound restrictive, but it served the people of that time and place. Understanding this deepens our appreciation for the challenges the Hebrew people faced as they sought to carve out a life in service to their God.

God of the ages, thank you for your people, who sought to serve you in faithfulness. Amen.

Wednesday, August 8
1 Samuel 12:6–16

*S*amuel gives his farewell speech to the Hebrew people,
ending his time of service as a judge and prophet of Israel.
Saul will now be king of Israel, marking the end of the time
of the Judges.

As Samuel bids the people farewell, he reminds them of the
great historic acts of God on behalf of the Hebrew people.
These acts make clear a central and repetitive biblical theme:
God provides. We know the stories; they remind us that God
provides food, land, and even a leader when the need arises.

Our worries are such that we often forget God's way of being.
We worry there will not be enough: enough money, enough
love, enough caring, enough health, and enough time. Just as in
ancient times, so it is now: God provides. Doubt may haunt us,
yet God is there. Samuel's message endures; it is a heartening
reminder of God's steadfastness then, now, and always.

*God, you are ever present. Help me to trust your care for me and
take my stand of faithfulness to you. Amen.*

*G*od is light; if we walk in that light, we have fellowship with one another and receive cleansing from sin by the blood of Jesus Christ. These are remarkable words.

We live in a world of wars and bullying and financial hardship. There is much fear because there seems to be much to fear.

These words, however, speak to a different reality: freedom, hope, and companions along the way. If we walk in God's way, we find fellowship with others who walk in the light. We are not alone. In addition, we find freedom from our sins.

Who wants to stay in the darkness when there is all this light, freedom, and companionship in God's way? Not I.

God, I confess my sins, trusting in your faithfulness to forgive me and cleanse me of unrighteousness. I seek to walk in your light and enjoy the company of other believers along the way. Amen.

This passage is very moving, beautifully expressed, and full of hope, even though a bit stern. Paul urges believers to stay the course, to persist in the faith. While the language he uses is a bit dour, he movingly describes the rewards of a faithful life.

This call to sobriety is meant to encourage an earnestly thoughtful life. The hope is that believers will carry out their ministry, be of service, share the faith, and endure what life brings their way. It is a recipe for any believer, whether in the first century or the twenty-first.

What is the reward of faithfulness? It is to become a libation, a living and sacred offering to God, poured out, holy and glorious. It is the reward for keeping the faith: service to Christ.

Holy God, strengthen my faith and conviction that I might fulfill my calling to serve in the world until I gain that crown of righteousness in the next. Amen.

*J*esus addresses the Pharisees, who question his right to make claims about himself. Jesus replies, "I know who I am."

Jesus comes from a place of deep self-understanding. He doesn't need to defend himself to the Pharisees; he reminds them that he knows himself well, and he lives and teaches in a manner that is true to self-knowledge. This deep-seated self-understanding contrasts with the Pharisees' refusal to acknowledge who Jesus really is or to listen closely to his teaching.

Jesus says to the Pharisees, "You know neither me nor my Father. If you knew me, you would know my Father also" (v. 19). He tells them that if they had any understanding of the God who sent him, they would understand what he was saying to them. Clearly, they know neither God nor Jesus. Thankfully, Jesus understands God, himself, and the people who seek him.

Jesus, who comes from our Father in heaven, lend me your understanding that I might live faithfully through you in this world. Amen.

*D*uring childhood, nicknames can be a way of finding identity. We want to stand out, be different, and (pardon the pun) make a name for ourselves. When I was younger, I tried different nicknames—shortening my name, using my middle name, or just going by an initial. I used these names to fit my personality; I eventually realized my first name fit perfectly.

We struggle with names for God. We call our Creator "Holy One" and "God," but we find these names are not enough—God is so multifaceted that no one name will suffice. Isaiah 9 shows yet another side of God—God is with the oppressed, fighting for justice and peace, providing a leader for peace. We name God Wonderful Counselor, Mighty God, Everlasting Father, and Prince of Peace. The mysterious and wonderful part is that God is so much more.

Limitless God, as we seek you, open our hearts to learn more about you, to learn who you are, and always to strive for peace. Amen.

*C*hristianity is a way of life. Even though we never reach perfection, we strive to be like Christ every day of our lives. This passage gives us a checklist to follow: righteousness, godliness, faith, love, endurance, and gentleness. Except we can never check all of these items off because we continue to strive for them and constantly seek God's will.

Paul must have known this, for he added, "Fight the good fight of the faith" (v. 12). It is an ongoing battle as we seek to be sanctified. Just when we think we have it right, something goes wrong. We are human, and we will mess up, but we are called not to give up following Christ and to trust that God is with us. God has called each one of us; we embrace the call and continue to seek righteousness, godliness, faith, love, endurance, and gentleness.

Almighty God, we try to be like Christ but fall short. Help us continue on the path that you have made for us, walking with us every step of the way. Amen.

*T*ransitions can be scary times. Those of us who are planners may be anxious about the unknown, but for those of us who live by the seat of our pants, the future can be exciting, bringing new adventures! I fall into the first category, with perhaps a splash of the second. I love new adventures but always want a plan.

First John assures us we have no need to worry. No matter what our situation—a congregation seeking a new pastor, an individual in a job transition, or a believer unsure where God is leading—we are reassured that we are children of God.

This amazing fact means that whatever the future brings, even beyond our lives, we will be with Christ, trusting that God is with us and walking with us every step of the way. We need not worry what the future brings because we are children of God, claimed by the Holy One.

Awesome Creator, we embrace being called your children and ask that you help us to act accordingly, following in Christ's path and trusting that you will be with us always. Amen.

*E*ach time I read this passage, I find it speaks an awful truth—"Violence takes lives away" (v. 30). It seems so obvious, like one of those warning tags on curling irons that say, "Hot! Do not touch!"

Sometimes I wonder if we need to be reminded; after five minutes of television or reading the front page of the newspaper, we can be overwhelmed by headlines about violence that ends in death.

This passage is more than just about the horror of violence; it is about recognizing from where abundant life stems. Violence and greed lead to loss—but God is the one who provides life. God is the source of existence; violence and greed take life away. Trusting in things that do not encourage peace and unity takes away life. We seek God and trust in the peace that God offers.

Gracious God, we ask for healing for those who have been hurt by violence. May your peace reign, and may we live in your abundant life, always seeking your love and wholeness. Amen.

I tried to imagine what it would look like to have walls of salvation, to be surrounded by salvation. I wondered what it would be like to be protected by peace and to see not because of light but because of God.

How would the world be if all were driven by righteousness and were to enter everything with praise? A physical picture of this might look a little silly; as a metaphor, the passage helps us to think outside the box—to see that God is not just creator but also illuminator.

Peace is not just a state of being; it is a protector. Metaphors help us to see beyond the ordinary. Sometimes we need that kind of vision in order to live as God calls us to live. We always look for solutions to problems in the church and in the world. Perhaps God is asking us to think in a new way and solve our problems through acts of righteousness while surrounded by salvation and guided by God.

God, may this text be our guide. Help us to reach out to others, knowing that we are protected by you and surrounded by you always. Amen.

*W*e may not all be singers, but certainly everyone has a way of praising God. Even when we sing, our voices don't have to be perfect; God wants us to act from our hearts.

Psalm 33 goes on to say that God loves justice. Many people probably would agree, but what does that mean? My justice may not be the same as your justice.

In a court of law, even jurors cannot always agree what justice looks like. Our justice system sometimes works, but there are a few flaws. Perhaps God's justice is not quite as we humans imagine it should be. Perhaps the human mind is not large enough to understand God's justice. But even if we cannot all agree, we know God is just, bringing peace to those who are hurting.

Forgiving God, you welcome all gifts, and we offer our best justice for you. May your justice be that which prevails. Amen.

*I*n seminary I heard many stories of how people had felt called to ministry for years but had fought it until finally they could procrastinate no more. Sometimes when God calls us, we drag our feet and turn our heads. Other times we are so grateful for what God has done for us that we simply cannot hold in our joy and the good news anymore. We want to shout it from the rooftops!

The psalmist has seen God's mercy and has been set free. Trouble has plagued the psalmist, but there is still hope. The author cries out to God, "I am your servant." There is a clear commitment because of trust in God.

No matter what God calls us to do, I pray that we may have the boldness of the psalmist and step up confidently, telling God, "I am your servant." May we be able to follow God's call with enthusiasm and grateful hearts, trusting God along the way.

Merciful God, even in difficult times you are with us. We are your servants. May we be examples of your love and justice in all of our actions. Amen.

*C*hristians interpret the branch that will spring up for David as Jesus. Moreover, the coming of Jesus means that the promises of God will be fulfilled. The new shepherd will gather the sheep, care for them, and keep them safe from harm.

Jesus has come; the Holy Spirit is with us; and still we struggle. There is, literally, no peace. What can we make of this?

There truly is a strength and a peace found only in God. "The Lord is our righteousness" is not an empty phrase; it is a promise fulfilled in day-to-day living. Rest in God's righteousness; do not be afraid, for God watches over the flock, caring for each one. The presence of Jesus Christ, through the Holy Spirit, is real and comforting, a source of strength in day-to-day life.

Help me, O God, to rest in the comfort of your watchful presence. May the knowledge of your fullness in my life give me strength and hope, day by day. Amen.

$\mathcal{P}$salm 23 has comforted believers through the ages. It is a familiar refuge. Read at funerals, services of remembrance, and Sunday morning worship, it has become part of the fiber of Christian tradition.

It is so powerful, in part, because it expresses such authentic human experience. We fear the unknown, becoming lost, being hungry or thirsty, being unloved. Here are the words that answer those fears: God guides us in the darkest time, giving us cool water, preparing the table, letting us rest, tenderly anointing us as God's own. Hardship and loss span the ages. Therefore, these words of promise and comfort remain as meaningful today as when they were first written.

"The LORD is my shepherd, I shall not want" (v. 1) is the answer to our prayers. The psalm tells us that God is present in our lives, remains concerned for our fears and losses, and will provide for our needs. In God, we find a place to dwell.

Ever-present God, your goodness and mercy are endless, providing me with a safe dwelling place. In you, my fear ends, allowing me to live fully in comfort and joy. Amen.

$\mathcal{G}$od speaks to Jacob in a dream. Jacob's family is full of conflict—his brother Esau despises him; his mother is in turmoil; and his father has sent him away to find a wife. As he travels to his uncle's home, he stops in the wilderness. He is between places, spiritually, emotionally, and physically. Jacob is sleeping in the open with his head on a stone, alone in the world.

It is in this place, in this lonely moment, that God comes to Jacob in a dream and speaks. God's words are as solid as the land on which Jacob sleeps, as real as the children who will be born to Jacob. "Know that I am with you and will keep you wherever you go," God promises (v. 15).

These promises, made to Jacob so long ago, are just as solid and real today. They are here, now, as God promises believers that God is with us, even now, ages later.

Our response to this can be as powerful as was Jacob's: "How awesome is this place!" (v. 17).

God of Jacob, help me rest in the assurance of your steady presence in my life. Help me live joyfully, knowing that you are with me wherever I go. Amen.

The promises of God have carried Jacob through his life—
promises of God's constant presence and God's intention to
build a people, a nation. Jacob has survived the loss of Joseph,
who was to be the keystone to the growth of the nation.

Despite this, Jacob persevered in hope that the promise
would be fulfilled. Late in life, he finds Joseph and his sons,
the promise of future generations fulfilled.

Jacob's faith in the promise of God carried him through times
of tremendous sorrow. His faith in the promise stems from
God's actions.

Reliance on God's activity, on the promise kept, is as true
today as it was for Jacob. God intends to be present for the
people of God; through Jesus Christ, that promise has been kept.

*God of generations, may I rely today on your truth in Jesus
Christ, who is your promise fulfilled. Amen.*

*G*od can lead us from our private Egypts. We all have them, for being human means experiencing loss. We are often held captive to grief, are oppressed by it, and struggle against it.

Yet God continues to be there, to desire our freedom and abundant life, to be the present "I AM" (v. 14). For the ancient Hebrew people, captive and suffering, this name meant an active and present God, real, alive, and vital. This activity and vitality bring hope to the people. This same activity and vitality bring hope to God's people still.

God is present in your life, in my life, and in the life of the church. God is I AM, capable of bringing us out of Egypt, out of oppression and hardship, out of hopelessness.

God of our ancestors, I put my trust in you. You desire my well-being, my freedom in you. Help me be open to your action in my life this day. Amen.

*M*y house lies in ruins, while all of you hurry off to your own houses," says God (v. 9). The temple has been plundered and burned. While the people of Judah are preoccupied with their needs, the house where God dwells is in ruins.

The image of a house in ruins suggests spiritual bankruptcy. People are so preoccupied with themselves that they neglect the center of the community's life. God calls the people to put their spiritual house—the temple—in order so that the community will thrive. By putting God at the center of life and concentrating on the difficult work of rebuilding the temple, the people of God will be grounded and know stability.

When we perform regular maintenance on God's temple, housed in our hearts, we thrive.

God of the people, help me today to maintain the inner temple and welcome you to dwell within me. Amen.

$\mathcal{J}$esus has been raised; the women find him and tell the others. Then Jesus appears to all of them and tells them to meet him in Galilee.

They gather there, in Galilee, the scene of some of Jesus' most profound ministry. Certainly, it is the site of his richest teachings. Now, in this postresurrection visit, Jesus has one last instruction for his disciples: Don't keep this to yourselves. Go and spread the good news that it might be of service to the world.

Thanks to those faithful few who followed that directive, here we are all these centuries later, assured that Jesus is with us always. Because we have him with us, we too follow the final command from the risen Christ: Go and tell the story; teach the ways of a faithful life; and know that Jesus is always, always with us.

Risen Christ, you comfort and strengthen me each day with your presence. Help me live faithfully into your teachings that I might know you and share you with a world in need. Amen.

*T*attered and torn from years of handling, the picture of the Good Shepherd held a treasured place on my grandmother's bedside table until the day she died. Night after night, as she snuggled herself into bed, my grandmother would gently hold the picture in her hands as she repeated the Twenty-third Psalm softly and rhythmically as a prayer of comfort and hope at the end of a long day.

Long before the time of Jesus, the prophet Ezekiel painted an image of comfort and hope for the people living in exile. Using an image from their daily life, Ezekiel shared God's words: "You are my sheep, the sheep of my pasture, and I am your God" (v. 31). The image of a shepherd assured the people of God's faithfulness and care in all situations. A shepherd is a protector, a guide, a caretaker, and a constant presence. God protects us, guides us, takes care of us, and is our constant presence.

What image of God brings you comfort and hope? How do you treasure that image and hold it close to your heart?

Shepherd God, help us feel your gentle arms around us as we rest in you. Amen.

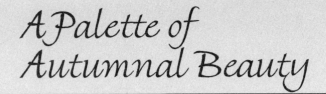

A Palette of
Autumnal Beauty

The scene was a familiar one—Jesus surrounded by crowds of people clamoring for his attention, his touch, his healing power. The centurion probably strode right through the crowd in Capernaum with an air of confidence and determination. A man of power, he did not stop until he came face to face with the one he had come to see. His request was quick and direct—his servant was in need of Jesus' healing power. Jesus' answer was predictable. He would come and cure the servant. What happened next was totally unpredictable and amazing (even to Jesus!). The authoritative centurion suddenly assumed a stance of humility.

How many times do we plow through the crowds with our agendas, ignoring the needs of others while asserting our interests? The story of the centurion and Jesus is an important one for us to hear, for only when we humble ourselves in faith before God can God's kingdom be accomplished on earth.

God of power and grace, create in me a humble heart and trusting spirit that rely on your power to heal a world in distress. Amen.

*P*aul was disappointed with his fellow Jews. They had become obsessed with rules and protocols of keeping the faith and were overlooking the basic tenets of belief in the Lord Jesus Christ. Sound familiar? How many committee meetings have been dominated by debates over protocol rather than the study of God's Word or proclamation of the gospel? How easy it is for us to cast stones!

Good teachers know the art of asking questions. Paul had been schooled in it as a student of the law. He lays it out simply and directly to his readers: "Everyone who calls on the name of the Lord shall be saved" (v. 13), regardless of race, station in life, or anything else! Then comes Paul's challenge, artfully laid out in a series of questions that prompt us, the students, to get back to the basics of proclaiming the Word.

Perhaps this passage should be read at the beginning of every church gathering! I wonder how the meeting would go if it were.

Savior God, keep our hearts and minds focused on your word rather than on our agendas and rules. Amen.

I cannot read verse 20 without bursting into a song I learned as a child! "It's no longer I who lives now, but Christ who liveth in me . . . in me . . . my Christ now liveth in me!" A simple chorus, designed to teach children Scripture, has become a great source of comfort and inspiration in my adult life.

My step is lighter, and my heart is filled with joy when I acknowledge the power of Christ in my life. I'm not left to my devices in living a faithful life of discipleship. I have an inward source of power that makes it possible for me, a sinner, to be made right with God. How amazing! How marvelous! How necessary it is to keep this song in my heart and mind in times when my faith is tested as well as in times when I'm filled with a sense of self-accomplishment.

I am not alone, and it is not about me—"It's no longer I who lives now, but Christ who liveth in me!"

Lord of life, fill me with your presence, and remind me that you live in me and provide for my salvation. Amen.

I hate shopping for clothes! Actually, the part I hate is standing in front of a mirror! Looking at myself, I instantly focus on all my flaws—too short, too wide (although I often refer to myself as "under tall" rather than "overweight"), too gray, and the list goes on. I do not relish Paul's challenge of deeply examining my life to see if I've passed the test of true discipleship. For when I look at myself in the spiritual mirror, I see even deeper flaws—too judgmental, too vocal, too quick to anger, and the list goes on.

Paul challenges us look in the mirror of faith to see how Christ shines through our lives. Imagine standing in front of a mirror that reflects the glory of Christ! Imagine seeing love, mercy, and grace instead of wrinkles and love handles. What a different look we would have if we saw beyond our flaws to the flawless face of Christ in the reflection!

God in the mirror, help me to see beyond the surface and into the grace-filled life you have promised. Amen.

*M*y mother used to say, "God won't send me more than I can handle—I just wish God didn't have so much confidence in me!" Her humorous declaration came from a deep faith in God's continued support and comfort in times of suffering and crisis. It was a faith that praised God in the good times and proclaimed God's promises in the bad times.

It's easy to sing praise to God when life is running smoothly, but Paul challenges us to proclaim God in times of suffering and crisis. No small order! For in times of suffering we are easily swept into a vortex of despair and hopelessness. Yet Paul reminds us that God's peace is with us in all times—good and bad—pouring love into our hearts through the Holy Spirit.

My mother clung to these promises in the final days of her life. She battled a consuming illness with an enduring faith that was filled with hope and God's peace. She proclaimed God's presence in her life throughout the good times and the bad.

Enduring God, fill me with your hope and peace in times of joy and in times of despair. Amen.

The Mission Yearbook for Prayer and Study, published annually by the Presbyterian Church (U.S.A.), is a fabulous resource. Designed as a daily call to prayer, the yearbook contains stories of God's amazing work across the denomination and around the world. It contains names of those who diligently spread the gospel message, stories of transformation, and Scripture readings. Those who read it are reminded of the marvelous ways we are interconnected as the family of God.

Paul kept his mission yearbook in his head. He remembered names of those who were at work for the gospel. He knew and appreciated the powerful support that came from prayer on behalf of others.

When we remember one another before God, give thanks for the work that God is doing, and ask for continuing support, we are engaged in the spiritual practice of building up the body of Christ. We are not alone in our work but rather a part of something much bigger than we are—the work of God!

Who will you remember and give thanks for today?

God of all, we give thanks for those who are working to spread the gospel message and build up the kingdom of God. Amen.

*O*ver and under, over and under! It was our first Sunday in a new church, and I had chosen to sit at the front so my children would be able to see better. My daughter sat dutifully attentive while my preschool son limberly slid over and under the pew in front of us like a gymnast warming up for the Olympics!

The choir worked hard to stifle their snickers while my husband, the new pastor, shot an occasional "evil eye" our way. With jaw clinched, I just wanted to make a quick getaway following the benediction, but suddenly, my little wiggle worm was scooped up by one of the largest men I'd ever seen.

Tossing my son into the air, this gentle giant proclaimed the most welcoming words I'd ever heard: "What a joy it is to have such energy in our worship service today! This little fellow is truly a window into the kingdom of God!"

Who will be your window into the kingdom of God today?

Loving God, help us to welcome everyone as Jesus did, and help us see your kingdom through the eyes of a child. Amen.

*A*t an early age, I was taught to sing "Blessed Assurance, Jesus Is Mine" with gusto and joy as a testament to the marvelous grace given by God through Jesus Christ. I can remember vividly the swell of the organ as the hymn reached its peak at the chorus. I can still feel the burn in my throat as I sang at the top of my lungs, "This is my story, this is my song, praising my Savior all the day long!"

Living in the full assurance of faith gives us the confidence to step into the world, proclaiming God's amazing grace and love for all people. It is this same faith that challenges us to be creative in the way we love one another, encouraging one another in Christ to tell the story and sing God's praises all the day long.

How will you sing your story?

Blessed God, fill us with Christ's goodness, and help us get lost in Christ's love. Amen.

*A*ccording to 1 Kings, Asa and his son Jehoshaphat were among the few kings of Israel who did what was right in the sight of the Lord. Second Chronicles gives a much fuller account of Asa's forty-one years. He began religious reforms that turned into a kind of wildfire revival. He drove heathen cults out of the land—even removing his grandmother as queen mother because of her idolatry. Asa also welcomed to Judah many refugees from Israel. Asa knew his kingdom looked small and weak in the sight of the surrounding enemies, but he kept his trust in the Lord God who would bring "peace on every side" (v. 7). Asa led the people to rebuild their city and their lives, keeping God at the center of it all.

When we keep God at the center of our lives and maintain our trust in God, we can gain strength in the face of our enemies. For in our weakness, God is strong. In our trust, God is revealed as sovereign and mighty.

In what ways is God the center of your life?

Powerful God, we offer you our lives in complete trust, knowing that you will do mighty and marvelous things. Amen.

I love the Psalms! Poems and songs that give voice to feelings with lyrics that cut right to the heart of every human emotion; hymns of praise, dirges of lament, prayers of hope, and proclamations of trust—all reminders of God's amazing power and love for those God created!

Psalm 3 gives voice to David's prayer of trust and reliance on his Lord God in the face of fear and adversity. Running for his life from his son Absalom, David prays aloud to God for security and peace in the face of his enemies:"God! Look! Enemies past counting! Enemies sprouting like mushrooms, mobs of them all around me!" (3:1, *The Message*).

Pleas for help uttered with complete trust in the Lord God to protect and save. How do we know that David had complete trust in God? David is so sure of God's protection that he lies down and sleeps! No, David doesn't sleep with one eye open—he sleeps with confidence knowing that God is there with him 24/7.

How many sleepless nights have you endured because of worrying about enemies who surround you?

Protector God, deliver me from those who want to do me harm and from the fears that prevent nights of peaceful sleep. Amen.

O Lord, hear my prayer. O Lord, hear my prayer. When I call, answer me. O Lord, hear my prayer. O Lord, hear my prayer. Come and listen to me." The words to this familiar Taizé hymn, written in 1982 by Jacques Berthier, could have been written by David in Psalm 4 as he proclaims his confidence and trust in God to deliver him from his enemies. Again, David shows his complete trust in God as he lies down prepared for a night of peace-filled sleep. He knows that he is completely safe from harm because God is watching out for him.

While our enemies may not chase us into the wilderness caves, they can haunt our dreams and sleep. Tossing and turning over words spoken in haste or sentiments left unexpressed can leave us staggering with fatigue. How different would our night's sleep be if we followed the pattern created by David? Try it next time your thoughts are haunting your sleep. Offer your prayer of trust, and allow the peace of God to cover you like a soft blanket, warmly and securely.

O Lord, hear my prayer. Come and listen to me. Amen.

*S*ynonyms for the word *trust* include *faith, belief, hope, conviction, expectation, reliance,* and *dependence.* Perhaps the most fitting synonym to describe David's triumphant song in Psalm 27 is *confidence!*

As a songwriter and poet, David's words capture the very heart of our faith when he sings, "The LORD is my light and my salvation; whom shall I fear?" (v. 1). Whether sung in Taizé-style or simply prayed in quiet tones, these words summon two very powerful images—a light and the cross—which are central for our faith. Jesus came as a light to the world living in darkness. Through Christ's death on the cross, the darkness was illuminated forever. As people of the light, redeemed through Jesus Christ, we can look forward to the time when we join God in the "house of the LORD . . . to behold the beauty of the LORD" (v. 4).

It's no wonder that David ended this passage with a song of praise. Who wouldn't want to sing and make melody to the Lord?

Redeemer God, we praise you this day for the light and salvation you brought into the world. We fear nothing, for we know that you are our God! Amen.

*P*atience has never been my strongest virtue! I shift my weight, look for the shortest line at the grocery store, and then tap my toe impatiently when the person in front of me has more than twelve coupons. I'm no different in my faith. I pray for God's will to be done and then try to make it happen. I pray for God to grant me patience and then plead for it to come now.

The second half of David's triumphant song of confidence pleads with God for continued guidance and support. It is a song that reminds us to wait for the Lord and to be strong while we wait.

When we trust in God, we allow ourselves to rely on God for the when, where, and how. Patience and trust take endurance, staying power, and fortitude. It's not an easy task, but it comes with the highest reward. For when we step aside and allow God to lead, marvelous things will happen!

Where in your life are you in need of patience?

Patient God, hear my prayer, and be good to me. Show me your goodness, and help me wait for you. Amen.

*M*y father loves sunsets! He plans his evening activities so that he can sit and watch as the sky fills with color and then fades completely from sight. Many are the times when I've heard him exclaim, "Wow, God—that was a good one!" Long ago, my father taught me about sunsets. Yes, I got the scientific lessons but always with the same preface—a sunset is a gift from God: a gift of beauty to enjoy, a gift of respite from the heat of the day, and a gift of time to be treasured.

Treasuring God's creation acknowledges God the creator of all that was, is, and ever will be. My father never viewed a sunset without a word of praise to God. While my father could explain the conditions that surrounded the sunset, he could not explain their origin—nor did he have to. The foundations of our faith are built on the acknowledgment that before there was anything, there was God! This foundation gives us assurance for life, provides a safe place in scary times, and sustains us in all things.

This week, watch a sunset or two, and give God praise!

God of life, remind us to treasure your creation and know that you are God. Amen.

I've often thought of the book of Job as a courtroom drama, full of long, eloquent speeches. For most of the book, Job sits in the defendant's chair listening to his friends' tirades. He knows no airtight refutations; what they say about suffering as punishment seems to make sense. Yet he also knows, deep in his soul, that they are wrong. He does not deserve the treatment he is getting. There has to be some other explanation. Like all grieving persons, Job goes through emotional cycles. He whines, explodes, cajoles, and collapses into self-pity. He agrees with his friends, then shifts positions and contradicts himself.

Eventually we all find ourselves in a position somewhat like Job's. Our world seems to crumble. Nothing makes sense any more. God seems distant and silent. At such moments of crisis, our faith in God is put on trial. Like with Job, well-meaning friends give rationalizations for suffering and offer encouraging words.

God alone will bind our wounds and offer healing.

How do you keep your faith in the midst of suffering?

Healing God, help us remain steadfast in your hands throughout the times of suffering. Amen.

*R*ecall the baptism scene in the movie *O Brother, Where Art Thou?* The sound of singing floats through the air until it reaches the ears of Delmar, Pete, and Everett. Curious, they go down to the river to investigate. Men and women in white robes file into the river to be baptized. The preacher calls for repentance.

Delmar suddenly runs head first into the river begging for redemption. Deep under the water he goes, only to emerge like a geyser, exclaiming, "I've been redeemed! The preacher done washed all my sins away! It's the straight and narrow from here on out!" Delmar stands before his friends, dripping wet, pledging to lead a new life as one who has been redeemed.

What a difference our lives would be if we would live as the "walking wet," keeping the cross of Christ in front of us and leaving sin behind in the river. Paul knew it was impossible for humans to live a sinless life, but he continually challenged his readers to bury their dead sin and live fully in Christ.

How do you live as one who is "walking wet"?

Redeemer God, show us how to be alive to Christ and dead to sin. Amen.

*T*he Olympics are amazing! Athletes from all over the world train for years for a single event. The track-and-field events have always fascinated me. I am in awe of the runners who walk onto the track and take their place alongside their competitors. Their muscles flex, hands twitch, and feet search for the placement on the track that will give them the best start. As the race begins, all the dedication, sacrifice, and training come down to a final second where one runner crosses the finish line and wins the gold medal.

Paul considered his whole life a race to the finish line where an eternal gold medal would be waiting for him. Like an Olympian-turned-coach, Paul challenges us to be diligent with our faith training so we can run hard, giving it all we've got! There's no time for sloppy habits and bad diets in Paul's training camp. A successful runner is dedicated to the race. What does it take to win? A diet of Scripture and a training schedule filled with acts of faithful discipleship.

How are you training for God's race?

Gold-medal God, inspire us to run with energy and endurance until we reach your finish line. Amen.

*T*here are no open machines at my gym during the month of New Year's resolutions. Newly committed men and women decked out in snazzy workout clothes sport the latest water bottles and ear buds. Zumba classes are filled to the brim, and herbal supplements fly off the shelves. People dedicate themselves anew to training regimens designed to drop pounds and tone muscles. Eventually, February comes, and the crowd thins; March arrives, and the gym is relinquished to the regulars.

Paul's message to Timothy was a March message: "Exercise daily in God—no spiritual flabbiness, please!" Workouts in gyms are useful, but a life filled with God is abundant and rewarding. This is not a quick weight-loss program that may succeed for a short time; it is a training regimen that will last a lifetime! It's easy to fall for the quick fix, but a life filled with the Holy Spirit will last longer, be fuller, and bring glory to God.

What does your daily workout with God look like?

Living God, strengthen our knees, and bring energy to our step as we strive to walk your path of righteousness. Amen.

*T*here is a reason that we plant lima beans or rye grass when we want to teach children about how things grow—we want something that grows fast and produces quick results! Our society continues to be obsessed with fast tracks and quick fixes. We want the solution now. We want the results yesterday.

"Be patient," James urges us as he offers a model of patient waiting. Farmers know that growth takes time and patience. It cannot be rushed. The seed matures in its own time as it is nourished by the rain and fed by the nutrients in the soil. The farmer cannot rush the process but must be patient to let nature take its course.

The Christian life needs slow nourishment that will provide growth toward full maturity. It is faithful endurance for the long haul, one that is steady and strong, that doesn't get caught up in judgment or other vices but rather seeks to honor God in all things.

How are you nourishing your faith for the long haul?

God of growth, be patient with us as we grow more fully into your ways. Amen.

*J*esus was not a wimp! I am offended by the movies and paintings that show Jesus as a meek and mild sufferer who walked through his ministry in a daze. In my mind, Jesus endured his suffering with assertiveness. He showed God's power and plan in the face of adversity and sin. Though he was treated like dirt, Jesus proclaimed God's acceptance of all people. Though he was despised and spat on, Jesus demonstrated love that knows no bounds. Though he was beaten and bruised, Jesus forgave and showed compassion on his abusers. Yes, Jesus endured much for our sake, and his faithfulness shows us that it can be done.

So suffer bravely, and never stop asserting the gospel. Christ's example is strong and set before us as a guide. Be encouraged in your times of doubt and strong in your times of weakness, for God is with you, undergirding your life with love and mercy.

How do you rely on God in tough times?

God of the faithful, help us rely on your strength and follow Christ's example in times of suffering. Amen.

The twelfth chapter of Hebrews reads like a coach's pep talk at halftime to a team in danger of giving up. "Strip down, start running—and never quit! Keep your eyes on Jesus, who both began and finished the race we're in. Study how he did it. Because he never lost sight of where he was headed—that exhilarating finish in and with God!" (12:2–3, *The Message*).

We all need to hear this pep talk from time to time when we are bogged down in the muck and mire of daily life. It's hard to see the cloud of witnesses that surround us when our eyes are lowered and focused only on our own steps. The writer of Hebrews encourages us to look up—beyond ourselves—to see God's path for our lives. Like a parent who walks in front of a child, God is there to lead the way for us. God does not provide an easy path but assures us of a constant guide who will never let go of our hands along the way.

How do you allow God to lead you?

God our guide, lead us in your ways along your path today and every day. Amen.

264

*T*he piercing siren of the hotel's fire alarm awoke me from one of my deepest sleeps. My mind went immediately to the boys in my youth group, wondering which one pulled the alarm. Dragging myself out of bed, I groped for my robe and headed into the hallway to find the nearest exit just in case it was a real alarm.

Ezekiel sounded God's piercing siren to the people of Israel. God's wrath would come upon the unjust if they didn't heed the siren and repent of their ways. How would God's people respond? It was up to them! Ezekiel, like the fire alarm in the middle of the night, only gave the warning. The safety of the people was placed in their own hands as they chose to respond to the alarm or not.

Alarms are essential to our safety, but the responsibility to heed their warning is in our hands. How will you respond to God's warning?

Merciful God, forgive us when we ignore the warnings you send our way. Amen.

The church has an ego problem. Set on doing the work of the Lord, we organize committees to budget and plan without stopping to listen first. We're so sure that we are right that we ignore the breath of God that is blowing in our midst.

John addressed church egos in his letters to the seven churches. The church in Sardis, for example, had the reputation of being alive and vibrant, yet they were dead inside. They were busy with the work, but the breath of God was not flowing through them.

God's gift of the Holy Spirit was sent to inspire, lead, and guide. So why don't we listen? Is it because we want to be leaders, not followers? Do we not realize that being a follower of God means allowing the Spirit to breathe life into our very souls? When we stop and listen first, we allow God's will to be done on earth as it is in heaven.

How do you allow the Holy Spirit to breathe through you?

"Spirit of the living God, fall afresh on me. Melt me, mold me, fill me, use me." Amen.

*W*hat's better—an original or a copy? Art collectors will tell you that an original is always a better choice. Although a copy can look amazing, it can never fully compare to the real thing.

According to Hebrews, the Old Testament rituals were a copy, but Christ is the original. The author pulls up time-hallowed images from the Jewish tradition—sacrifices, laws, blood, the tabernacle, the priest, the day of atonement—and explains how Christ revealed once and for all the meaning at which these images only hinted. The incomplete, shadowy copy contrasts with the perfect, genuine reality. Because of Christ, sacrifices are no longer necessary, and God's laws are now written in our minds and on our hearts, not in a formal code. "It is finished," Christ cried out from the cross. God's covenant was complete.

Through Christ, our covenant with God provides knowledge of our past, guidance for our present, and hope for our future. Through Christ, we have the freedom to live as those who have been redeemed for a purpose.

How do you value God's covenant in your life?

Redeemer God, thank you for the gift of your Son and for the covenant with you. Amen.

*T*hank you." Two simple words with a complexity of meaning. As a young child, I was taught to say, "Thank you" to anyone who paid me a compliment or gave me a gift. "What do you say?" still rings in my ears as my mother sought to instill in me a heart of gratitude for the kindness and generosity shown to me by others.

When we offer the simple words of thanks, we acknowledge the person who is serving or giving. We recognize their effort and show appreciation for their intent. I was told to say "thank you" even when I did not appreciate the gift. For in offering thanks, I was honoring the value of the giver rather than the gift.

Everyone needs to hear a thank-you from time to time. For those who labor for Christ, these simple words, spoken in earnest, can lift a weary soul and bring confidence to a shaky spirit.

How will you thank someone today for his or her efforts for God's kingdom?

Thank you, God, for the gifts of those who seek to spread your gospel and tell your story. Amen.

$\mathcal{J}$esus loved to turn things upside down! Everyone knows you should love one another, but it's not enough to love the loveable ones—Jesus wants us to love the unlovable ones as well! Now, we've got a problem. Our human nature wants to choose to whom we show love. After all, we can't be expected to like everyone we meet—can we? What about the spiteful ones who look down their noses at us as we walk by? What about the passive-aggressive ones who keep us off balance in our work?

Jesus didn't offer us an option on this one! Jesus turned things upside down when he said, "Love your enemies and pray for those who persecute you" (v. 44). Jesus challenges us to love with God's love, not ours. We respond to others with kindness and energy that is born of prayer. Jesus challenges us to live as grown-ups, generously and graciously toward others, the way God lives toward us.

Offer prayers today for those you love with God's love— friends and enemies.

Loving God, show us how to love with your love, and help us live out Christ's challenge. Amen.

I made an ill-fated decision, one Fourth of July, to climb to
the top of Montreat's Lookout Mountain with my husband and
three young children. "Come on, Mom, it will be fun!" they said.
"We'll help you!" they promised. I climbed—without hiking
shoes, without a water bottle, without a full understanding of
what "climbing Lookout" meant! By the time we got to the top
of the mountain, I was drenched with sweat and breathing
heavily. My knees were weak; my feet were blistered; but
my children were giddy with joy as we made it to the top!
We sat on the rocks for a long time enjoying a sight that was
only visible to those who had climbed the mountain. It was
spectacular!

God's calling to a life of discipleship is not for the weak.
Sometimes it's a hard climb up a steep mountain. However,
the view from the top is spectacular—one that is shared with
our God, who loves us enough to go before us as our guide
and behind us with words of encouragement for our "drooping
hands and weak knees."

What mountain of faith are you climbing?

*Encouraging God, give us strength for the long haul so that we
can pursue peace and holiness. Amen.*

You didn't hear the alarm clock and overslept. It seems impossible to find clothing that isn't hopelessly wrinkled or two shoes that match. Car keys are nowhere to be found; you forgot your umbrella, and now it's storming. Everyone in your house is especially cranky this morning as you bark that you have to leave right this minute or you're going to be late for church. My grandmother used to say that the devil worked overtime on Sunday mornings.

Sometimes it is an uphill battle just to get to church, much less to enter our worship spaces with any sense of awe and wonder. We're just happy to have made it there in one piece (more or less). Yet Hebrews reminds us of a God who cannot be shaken, even in our shaken-up world. God is in the blazing fire, the blasting trumpets, and the blinding chaos of our days. In the midst of all that is going on, God says, "Come, and find peace." Indeed, we worship this God!

God of compassion, consume us with your grace, and create in us open spaces to receive your kingdom and respond in worship. Amen.

I love you, O LORD" (v. 1). More than simply uttering these powerful words, the psalmist frames love for God through thanksgiving, highlighting the diverse ways that God has shown love. God has given the psalmist strength in times of distress, has been the listening ear and protective arm, has been in constant loving relationship with God's people. Now the psalmist has the opportunity to respond in love.

How do you show love? Do you share it with notes of care or statements of adoration? Do you show it through kind gestures or time spent together? Are you the giver who always finds just the right gift? We all have different ways of demonstrating care. In fact, entire books have been written to analyze these different ways. Consider the different relationships in your life and the different ways love manifests itself in each of these unique bonds.

Consider your relationship with God. How are you showing love there?

God of strength, you are our rock, fortress, and deliverer. May we move, day by day, closer in relationship with you. May we have the boldness of the psalmist to say, "I love you, O LORD." Amen.

*W*hen I was a child, my parents instituted a sticker-chart reward system. Every time I made my bed in the morning, emptied the trashcans, or practiced the piano, I got a sticker on the corresponding row in the chart. After a specified number of stickers, an appropriate reward was given. It made sense, working for something and then being rewarded. While good in some areas, the sticker-chart idea doesn't work when it comes to love. No amount of dishes cleared from the table would earn what I already knew I had been given—the love of my parents.

If God had a sticker chart, we'd all be in trouble. Deuteronomy reminds us that nothing we have done, no amount of stickers, can earn us God's love. Rather, God's love comes from a faithfulness that was promised to countless generations of God's people. It is a covenantal love, given freely. It is a love that is not fleeting but everlasting. It is a love in which God says, "I have filled your sticker chart with grace. Come receive my love."

Thank you for your reckless love and abundant grace, O God, especially when we cannot earn it. Amen.

Before playing a game or putting together a project that comes in pieces, most of us take the time to look at the instructions. We identify which pieces go where, what other tools we might need, and which step comes first. The instructions set the stage for what comes next and focus us on the task. If we hit a snag, they give us something to which we can return. The same is true of the Ten Commandments. These words orient us to how we are to approach our lives with God and with one another. The foundation of fulfilling the commandments is fidelity to God.

It may seem an easy task at first glance, and sometimes it is, but we know that idols take their place as our first love. Competition for our resources of time, money, and energy challenge our ability to obey this simple commandment, giving us the opportunity to state clearly, from the beginning, whom we will serve. God shows steadfast love to us, is with us throughout the generations, and calls us into obedient love.

God of the covenant, continue to bind our hearts to you in love, that we, obeying your commandments, may follow you. Amen.

*K*nit one. *Purl one. Knit one. Purl one.* Inch by inch the yarn is carefully knit into a scarf or blanket. The end of the row is reached, and the pattern begins again. *Knit one. Purl one.* These basic movements are the building blocks of knitting. We learn these first, followed by practice. We create simple lines of scarves and eventually more complex cable patterns. The key to success is repetition and rhythm, which along with an awareness of the pattern give way to more than just yarn knotted together. Knitting is a discipline and a joy, teaching not only a craft but also a way of being in the world.

Knitting and other activities of repetition gives us insight into how we are to approach our love of God. We are to learn the basic steps, to focus on loving God with all of ourselves: heart, soul, and might. Then we are to practice these steps, day by day, with a disciplined rhythm that leads to something new, our lives woven in the yarn of God's love so intimately that we are unable to live any other way. We are taught to love. One step at time.

Creative God, weave us together into new creations that speak of your love. Amen.

*I*t wasn't because of the fish decal on the back of her car. It wasn't because of the crosses hanging around her neck and dangling from her ears. It wasn't because they saw a bulletin tucked into the side of her purse. It wasn't even because they saw her pause for a split second in prayer before beginning to eat. It wasn't because of anything she said. But they knew she was a Christian.

They knew by the smile she gave to the homeless man who was begging near the entrance, how she paused on her way to look him in the eye and speak with him. They knew by the warm exchange and lively conversation she had with the friend she was meeting. They knew by the extra seat that was pulled up to their table: a third guest had been invited to their meal. They knew because everything she did reflected care for others.

"And they'll know we are Christians by our love, by our love, yes they'll know we are Christians by our love."

Holy One, may we move from complacent Christianity into lives of devoted discipleship that radiate your love; through Jesus Christ, our Lord, Amen.

*W*ould you do me a favor?" From watering plants to making a special phone call, we are all apt to agree to small favors for friends. The closer the relationship, the greater or more frequent the favors. It's a part of being in relationship with one another, and most of us don't mind helping one another out every now and then. What happens, however, when the one asking the favor is not our favorite person, or is one we dislike greatly— an enemy? Excuses are easier. Schedules are suddenly full, and contacts seem to turn up missing. "No" slips easily off our tongue.

Jesus' words state what we already know—it is easy to help those whom we like but harder to be kind to our enemies. We are challenged to do something other than accept this as reality and instead do what is harder, namely, to love our enemies. The road of discipleship is a harder path, to be sure. It calls us to reject the world's standards of favors and favorites and to let God's standard of mercy guide us.

Where there is hatred and when "No" is on our lips, Lord, give us pause to remember your mercy, that we might be transformed to love those who are hard to love. Amen.

*I*mages of weddings swirl around these words from Paul about what love truly is. The Hebrews text even speaks to the importance of mutual love and will later reference marriage explicitly. As true and applicable as these texts are to marital relationships, they are by no means limited to them.

Both writers speak of something more than romantic love. Their language is a clue. In 1 Corinthians 13, the Greek word *agape* carries a connotation of deep, sacrificial love, much like God's love for humankind. In Hebrews, the Greek word *philadelphia* describes a love between close friends characterized by loyalty and virtue. In each instance, the authors call their respective communities into more intimate relationships with one another, relationships in which joys and burdens are shared, faith is deepened, and hope comes alive.

So we, too, are called. We are to model God's love to one another and to those strangers in our midst through hospitality, broadening the wide circle of God's love in a community that seeks to see more clearly the splendor of God's grace.

God of love, open our hearts to one another. Let mutual love surround all our relationships. Amen.

*O*ur experience of faith is often depicted as a journey, although it's not always a walk in the park. You duck under low-hanging tree branches, brush away spiderwebs, and step over puddles. The winding road ends at a powerful stream with only a few slippery rocks on which to find your footing. Does your faith journey ever feel like an obstacle course?

Exiled from their home, persecuted, and facing judgment, the Israelites knew firsthand the obstacle course of faith. Naturally, they began to wonder where God was. Did God not hear them? Did God not care? The prophet Isaiah offers a rationale: God has not been absent. Rather, the Israelites have gotten in their way with self-made obstacles of sin, injustice, and violence.

The barriers that come between God and us make our paths more treacherous. We call them sin. In confession, we humbly bring them before God and one another, trusting that we worship a merciful God who will cleanse and forgive us. May we be so bold as to acknowledge our obstacles to God and one another and to seek other paths!

Merciful God, remove that which keeps us from you, and replace our obstacles with paths that lead us to justice and righteousness. Amen.

*S*ticks and stones may break my bones, but words can never hurt me." This taunting playground rhyme sounds good when one is faced with a schoolyard bully's verbal attack, but ultimately it doesn't ring true all the time. The harsh reality of our world is that words hurt. The bending of the truth, the twisting of words, or flat-out lies can leave us deeply wounded. They rattle our trust and raise our walls of suspicion as we hide our tears. We become cautious of everyone in a different way than before, not sure whom we can believe.

This is the pain found in today's passage: a voice longing for justice and security. We hear the crying out for healing as from that medicinal balm found in the region of Gilead.

We are not alone in the suffering. God is also grieving with us, longing for honesty, justice, and healing.

In a world of hurt, Lord, send your healing balm. Restore our trust, and surround us with truth. Amen.

*I*n a world of options, many are perceptive comparison shoppers. We analyze packaging and advertising, noting claims about the benefits of a particular brand. Consumer magazines and Internet reviews make it easy to learn about a product before we purchase it. Why do we make such an effort? We know that in the marketing game not every boastful claim can be true.

What if all we knew were truth? What if we lived in a world that heeded God's word in Zechariah? It would affect far more than our shopping habits. Such a world would be jarring. Good or bad, words and actions could be taken at face value. Market research, second-guessing, and game playing would no longer be necessary. Imagine what we could do with our time.

Speaking the truth to one another might also lead us to walk more in God's truth, the truth Zechariah describes in verses 15 and 19. God seeks to do good for God's people and welcomes us into seasons of joy and gladness.

God, speak your truth to us, that we might live into that truth and be at peace. Amen.

*I*n *Bambi,* Thumper is reminded of a valuable lesson: "If you can't say something nice, don't say nothing at all." Such words of wisdom guide the rambunctious young bunny into a way of living that uplifts. As we live into Thumper's mantra, we often slip into those little white lies that allow us to illustrate the first part, so we are at least saying something nice.

Proverbs 8 offers an edit to this catchy line: "If you can't say something *true,* don't say anything at all." Verse 5 calls us to pursue prudence and intelligence, as we discern when and when not to speak. Beauty comes in the words of truth; righteousness and praise follow from noble things spoken. Here is the wisdom by which we should strive to live. As we learn to speak the truth, perhaps it's not a bad idea for us to pause and reflect on what we are being called to say.

God of wisdom, help us to learn prudence, acquire intelligence and discretion, and speak truth in wisdom. Amen.

*A*s we search for truth, for direction, we can do a lot of things—from making lists of pros and cons to conducting in-depth research—but in the end we come up short. We need something greater than we are, a guide, to help us. We need a God who is present and active in our lives. John reminds us of a God who lived and breathed with us through Jesus Christ. We hear Christ's promise that God's Spirit will be with the disciples as a guide. Jesus assures the disciples, and us, that we don't have to do it alone.

With this assurance, we eagerly listen for the wisdom of God's Spirit to lead us. To welcome the Spirit's presence, we must create space in our lives. Through prayer, Scripture, and spiritual discipline we create that space. Through spoken word in holy conversation and moments of quiet and stillness, the Spirit surrounds us. The Spirit is our Advocate and Counselor, who pokes and prods us to open our minds, hearts, and souls to where God would have us go.

Spirit of God, fill us with your presence, and guide us into all truth. Amen.

*C*hurch bulletins and newsletters often list ministers as "all members of the church," boldly claiming that all are called and equipped by God to serve. As individuals, though, we are quick to come up with lists of how we are not qualified to serve.

In Acts, the seven who are chosen are not selected because of outstanding culinary expertise or service records. Rather, they are qualified because they are "of good standing, full of the Spirit and of wisdom" (v. 3). Their service is marked with prayer and the laying on of hands. They are blessed by the community, which trusts that God will continue to fill their vessels to overflowing.

God has a lot of work for us—the work of ministry. Whether we are busing tables at a fellowship dinner or leading the study of Scripture, we are called into service. We are equipped and filled through the worship of God, who promises that our cups are never empty, even when we view them as half full. Through God, we have fullness.

Empowering God, fill our cups to overflow with your grace, that we may hear your call and minister in your name. Amen.

*H*ere we find Stephen, full of grace and power, spreading the good news of Jesus Christ among the people. He is busy preaching, but, as it goes when faced with Truth, not everyone is happy with him. Some stood up to him. Still others argued against him. In the face of opposition, Stephen speaks with wisdom and gives thanks for the presence and power of the Holy Spirit.

It is a wonderful snapshot of life lived in the Spirit. Stephen rests in the grace and wisdom of God that is poured out on him. He doesn't worry about what others are thinking or even the consequences of his forthright speech. He trusts in the power of the Spirit.

This same grace and power is given to each of us to face life's challenges. Life in the Spirit is not so much about living free of fear as it is about facing fears with trust. Trust in the power and presence of the Spirit to be with us and see us through: this is the life of faith, given to us in Jesus Christ.

God, I thank you for your gifts of grace and power, present in my life. May I live my life this day, confident in the presence of your grace to face whatever challenges today may bring. Amen.

*P*ray in the Spirit at all times in every prayer and supplication"
(v. 18). Paul urges readers to attend to their prayers. We are
blessed to have a form of communion with God that is available
at any time. As we live our lives, day by day, prayer can be a
constant for us. At any time and in every place, we may simply
open our hearts to God and offer ourselves and our work for
God's blessing and intervention.

This God-given grace is available to us at any time but
is difficult to practice. We become caught up in business, in
urgent tasks, in pressing matters, and forget that God is simply
a breath away. God is always here, listening for us, waiting to
hear our needs, and drawing us close. In the richness of grace,
we need only pause and offer to God our next moment, our
next task, and our next concern to be lovingly received by
our listening God.

*Listening God, help me on this day to offer you my concerns
many times throughout the day. Let me rest assured you wait
for me and hear my prayers. Amen.*

*T*oday we read from Stephen's speech before the council, defending himself and the good news he preaches. As he builds his case, he reviews salvation history—the story of God's saving actions on behalf of the people of God.

Stephen reminds us that God keeps promises. In the fullness of time, the promises will be fulfilled according to God's way, not as we may have decided those promises ought to be fulfilled.

Day to day we can rest assured that God keeps promises. They may not be what we expect. The people and circumstances involved may be different from how we envision them. God keeps promises, promises to love, to be present with us, to comfort and to save. Our God keeps promises.

God of steadfast presence and mercy, help me rest on your promises, knowing you are with me, a present help in my life. Amen.

$\mathcal{M}$oses meets God in the Sinai wilderness and is commanded to take off his shoes, for he stands on sacred ground. Each moment of each day, we encounter God in such a way. God is readily available to us; we can see God if we will pause and open ourselves to the Holy Presence. We, too, "remove our shoes" by acknowledging God's presence with us.

In this way, we stay connected with God regardless of what our day holds. Pause in the moment, and savor God's presence. Then pledge your gifts to be used by God. For God sends us, just as God sent Moses, into the world to be of service and care to others. Without this vital God connection, we have little to give. With this ongoing connection we, too, are sent by God near and far to be of aid.

So pause in the moment. Take off your shoes, for you stand on holy ground. Now go and serve the God who has sent you.

God of the burning bush, I stand before you today and ask that you use me in service to others. Amen.

*I*n this passage, Stephen continues giving the salvation history of God's interaction with the people of God. It is clear in his speech that God has steadily and faithfully been present throughout history. What is also clear is that God's people have not always been as steady or as present.

God's people can be fickle. What underlies our fickleness is fear. When we become afraid, we tend to turn toward the sure thing even if that sure thing is a small bit of bread clothed in the garb of slavery. The people yearned for Egypt and a steady, if poor, diet rather than wandering in the wilderness, unsure of food to eat or water to drink and with only Moses as guide.

There are times when God's way is the wilderness way. We don't know the path; there is no roadmap; and sustenance is hard to come by. Even in those circumstances, in the midst of mystery, there is freedom and God's presence to give us hope.

God, there are times when I feel I have lost my way. Help me rest in the assurance that your presence and guidance are steadfast and sure. Amen.

The people have been following Moses, wandering in the wilderness, searching for their promised land. Yes, they have escaped Egypt and endless slavery and misery. Yet they are restless, uncertain, and ready to get there already.

Wandering in the wilderness is no fun. It brings uncertainty, insecurity, and anxiety over the next meal. The question "How much farther?" hangs in the air; grumblings over Moses' incompetence are constant. Rather than endure so much uncertainty, in their hearts the people turn back toward Egypt. They choose to claim the certainty of a small meal and ready expectations rather than endless wilderness wanderings.

One must trust in God one day at a time, living in the now, in community, taking a step at a time through the wilderness toward a promised land. It isn't easy. It is often tempting to turn back toward the known and toward "slavery," which may take the form of addiction, consumerism, or even faith in country over trust in God. No matter the form, slavery is not the way to freedom.

God, help me to take your hand and wander on in the wilderness rather than turn my heart back to Egypt. Amen.

God is not confined to the temple. If we focus too closely on the temple as the location for God, we tend to focus on the building rather than the Being.

Stephen reminds us that God is everywhere and cannot be confined. The building is more for us than for God. Our church building gives us a place to gather as the community, to worship together, and to build relationships. It is a tool to enhance our faith expression, but it is not the only place to meet God. God is present everywhere: in the comfort we offer a neighbor, at the dinner table as our family gathers, in the woods as we wonder at the owl we see.

The only limitations on God's presence are those we place on God. Stephen reminds us of this when he says, "The Most High does not dwell in houses made with human hands . . ." (v. 48).

Ever-present God, may I pause this day, wherever I am, and take a moment to be mindful of you. Amen.

*W*hen things are going our way, it is much easier to claim a powerful God than when life shoots trouble at us. Isn't it ironic, though, that great adversity can also stir in us great faith? Take Stephen, for example. When we meet Stephen in Acts 7, he has a mess of trouble on his hands. I wonder what thoughts crossed his mind as he awaited trial before the Sanhedrin. Did he pray for rescue, or was he resigned to the death he faced at the hands of his accusers?

We do know this: when every shred of reason would indicate a humble defense, Stephen steps up and boldly proclaims his conviction that the God of Israel was the same God who sent Jesus into the world. The God of power who called Abraham, Moses, Aaron, Joshua, David, and Solomon was the same God who opened the heavens to receive the ascended Christ. This same God opened the heavens again to welcome Stephen. Stephen's testimony speaks of his spiritual ancestors, a story into which God has written our lives.

Will we stand with those who are for Christ? Or will we stand with those who oppose Christ? How we choose will be reflected in the kind of lives we live.

Gracious God, lead us through the valley of shadows. Amen.

*B*ildad thought he understood God's power, but Job's response exposes the fallacy of human attempts to explain the manner in which God exercises power. It is beyond words! Beyond understanding! We cannot grasp God's power, and any attempt to do so proves futile.

Job makes the point by comparing the enormity of God's power to a devastating thunderstorm and concludes that the force of the storm is a faint whisper of God's potential. Like Bildad, we may try to wrap life's difficulties in neat packages under the pretense of making sense out of them, but it does more harm than good. We are actually more receptive to the Spirit's movement in our lives when we are willing to accept life's messes. Rather than forcing God to fit into a box built by us, we can open ourselves to a more intimate knowledge of God when we accept the unpredictability of storms. In the very moment that we admit we cannot know, we find an infinite God who gives a gift of understanding.

O God, help us to hear the faint whisper of your love and compassion in the storms of life. Amen.

*W*e learn from the seven sons of Sceva that it is a mistake to throw about the name of Jesus as though it were some super incantation to dispel the trouble we're in. The power that resides in the name of the Lord isn't released through Latin pronunciations or specially formulated spells. There is a person attached to the name, and it is only in building a relationship with Jesus that I am invited to pray in his name and according to his authority.

Imagine flipping through a phone book and calling up the first person on whose name your finger lands. The person answers and you say, "Hey, I'm having car trouble; can you come and help me?" There's a slim chance the stranger will come, but the odds of your finding help are far better if you call up a friend with whom you've built a relationship over many years.

Praying in Jesus' name is a gift reserved for those who call him friend.

O Christ, thank you for embracing us as friends. Give us the courage to invite others into your circle of friends. Amen.

*T*he cross does not make any sense to those who are "perishing," but for those who are "being saved" the cross holds wisdom and power.

What do these two poles represent? The perishing are those who put their trust in earthly wisdom. Those who are being saved are the ones who hear in Christ's message the wisdom of God, even when Christ was nailed to the cross. The utter irony of God's power is that it is revealed in the powerlessness of Christ crucified.

The most highly educated Jewish scholars were experts on signs. The most highly educated Greeks were expert philosophers. Paul tells the Corinthians that God's wisdom confounds the most educated in society because confidence in their brilliance blinds them to a proper awe and respect for God. Just because we have the benefit of hindsight, we should not be too quick to assume that we have a perfect understanding of God's ways. Knowing God does not depend on how many books we've read or where we went to school. The humble in heart are most receptive to God's wisdom and will therefore inherit an understanding of Scripture.

God of wisdom, give us eyes to see your power through weakness. In Christ's name. Amen.

*W*e have access to infinite sources of information that surround us in our everyday lives. We watch 24-hour cable news networks, listen to the radio, subscribe to the local newspaper, and surf the Internet. Even though information is available 24/7, there is a downside.

We consume information almost as if it were food necessary for survival. An accumulation of knowledge may give us some sense of control over our lives, but if Paul's words to the Corinthians are true, then all of the knowledge in the world will not do us one bit of good in terms of moving us toward righteousness, holiness, and redemption.

If we are concerned to live in harmony with God's wisdom, then we need to approach life in a countercultural way. It doesn't mean that we close ourselves off from the world but that we filter the information that comes to us through the lens of who we are in Christ. We weigh all that we know or think we know in the balance against the wisdom of God.

Bless us, O God, with ears to hear and eyes to see the truth of your amazing love. Amen.

*S*in can sneak up on us in a clever disguise. It can impersonate a good cause, a pat on the back, or some well-intentioned opportunity. If sin presented itself to us as ugly and unattractive, then we'd quickly recognize it and run the other way. Most of the time sin is so insidious that we're drawn in for a closer look.

Thankfully, we do not have to fend for ourselves. God provides the Spirit to help us in our weakness and expose the lies so that we can see sin for what it really is. When we follow the guidance of the Spirit, we better discern right and wrong, good and evil, God's way and sinful ways.

A simple test for discerning the way of the Spirit is to ask, "What is the loving thing to do?" Or you could use John Wesley's rule to do no harm. Either approach will expose sin's deceit and lead you on the right path. Trust the Spirit, and you won't go wrong.

O Spirit of truth and goodness, guide our steps away from sin and toward the perfect way of Christ, in whose name we pray. Amen.

*H*ow might we achieve world peace? We could start small and say that every person will treat every other person with love, joy, peace, patience, kindness, goodness, faithfulness, gentleness, and self-control. From there we could spread our circle and say that every member of the church will extend the fruits of the Spirit to every other member. Once we saw the fruits of the Spirit at work in our congregation, we could extend the plan so that every Christian would commit to treating every other Christian in the world with love, joy, peace, and all the rest. A simple plan.

What if we got so excited about the plan that our enthusiasm spread to people of other faiths? And people of no faith? Soon every person in the whole world would be treating others with love and respect. It sounds too good to be true! Dare we believe when we pray, "Thy kingdom come; thy will be done on earth as it is in heaven" that it could really happen? Galatians 5 says, "Dare to believe that it will begin with me."

God, pour out your Spirit on the whole world, beginning with me, and let me be your servant in Christ's name. Amen.

*M*oney can buy many things, but the Holy Spirit is not one of them. Peter rebuked Simon the sorcerer quickly when he offered money to obtain the power to give the Holy Spirit through the laying on of hands. Peter's rebuke says it all: "May your silver perish with you" (v. 20).

God is the giver of the Holy Spirit. The best gifts cannot be bought with money but are given from the hand of God. Recent television ads have targeted a list of some of the amazing things that money cannot buy. The list includes relationships with family and friends, sunsets, time spent with someone you love, memories, and more. The ad ends with the notion that some things money cannot buy; for everything else, you can use a credit card.

Even our consumerist society cannot put a price tag on the gifts from God. What priceless gifts do you hold? Give thanks to God for them today, and praise God from whom all blessings flow.

Great God, I give thanks for the priceless gifts that you have bestowed on my life. Amen.

*H*ow far do you have to travel before you see a billboard, commercial, or magazine ad or hear an announcement about the newest way to become blemish free? We have facials, fillers, removers, implants, extracts, and surgery to clear up our blemishes. Blemishes are inherent to humans.

Leviticus 21:16–24 lists physical infirmities under the category "blemishes." These include things that are beyond our control, such as blindness, disfigured limbs, broken bones, eczema, and even a scab. The Lord told Moses that anyone who has a defect shall not approach or come near the offerings made by fire to the Lord. In the same breath, these people should not be mistreated or starved. They are invited, blemishes and all, to eat the bread.

We are broken and blemished people. The Lord is the one who will sanctify those who eat the bread of God. An outward blemish might draw attention, but the work of the Lord is completed on the inside. That is where our true beauty and wholeness lie. Our sanctity comes from the Lord. God never excludes us but feeds us from the abundance of the Lord. Praise be to God.

O God, wash me, and I will be clean. Feed me with the bread of life that I may rejoice in your presence. Amen.

*E*veryone in the school was invited to watch the seniors launch a rocket they built. Classes began to gather at the top of the hill.

One student had been left at the bottom of the hill because his teacher thought it would be too hard to push his wheelchair to the top. Three of my students took it upon themselves to push, pull, lift, and carry him until he had the same view as everyone else. They did it! The only time they looked down at the student was when they were lifting him up.

Jesus began his ministry speaking to the crowds about how God had sent him to fulfill the good news. God had anointed him to preach good tidings to the poor and heal the brokenhearted. God heals the brokenhearted and binds up their wounds; God counts the stars and knows them all by name. The Lord lifts the humble. How beautiful it is when we sing and praise God while helping someone see from a different vantage point! Does someone near you today need to be lifted to see Christ? Be the hands and feet of Christ today in the world.

O God, lift our eyes to your glory as we reach down to answer your call to help the poor and oppressed. Amen.

*W*ho can forget the times in middle school or high school when your class was to divide into teams? Human nature drives us to want to be captain of the team. If not, we surely don't want to be the last choice.

No matter what the reason or the cause, someone, somewhere right now is feeling like an outcast. Isaiah speaks of salvation for the Gentiles. The Lord says, "Maintain justice, and do what is right, for soon my salvation will come, and my deliverance be revealed" (v. 1). The gathering of the outcasts mentioned in this passage is affirmed through Jesus' ministry. God acknowledges them as important. God takes seriously that God's "house shall be called a house of prayer for all peoples" (v. 7). God takes seriously the "all" part in God's people and the importance of prayer for all people. God gathers all, including the outcasts.

Let us prayerfully cover all people, outcasts included, with God's love.

Holy God, you sanctify all people in your love and mercy. Help me to recognize my neighbor as your beloved child. Amen.

*M*y husband and I loved volunteering at our children's school. Our highlight was Track-and-Field Day. The parent volunteers were there to encourage, run stopwatches, measure distances, and cheer the children to compete and complete to their very best.

There's nothing like a cheering squad to help everyone across the finish line. Encouragement and praise can spur us to cross the finish line when we are exhausted and struggling to catch our breath.

God rejoices over each of us with gladness. God rejoices over us with singing and quiets us with love. We get exhausted, worn out, and fall short of God's glory all the time. When shame or doubt overshadows us, we run out of strength and perseverance. That is the exact time that we see the Lord cheering us on to victory. When shame takes your breath away and leaves you depleted, rejoice in the breath and grace of God. Our limitations and weaknesses allow God to shine and be our strength.

Let God delight in you and cheer you to victory.

My God, guide my feet; run the race with me; and let me hear your encouraging words. For without you, I am lost. Amen.

A refugee family has come to live in our community. On the run and constantly on the move, they carried their shelter with them. It consisted of several sheets of plastic. Now, they live in a home with a roof over their heads and walls surrounding them. They worship, live, and work in our community, which they now call home.

God is our shelter and protects us from the face of the oppressor. The One who sits on the throne of truth will execute God's gracious mercy. Isaiah speaks of a new government of love, with a ruler who is passionate for justice and quick to set things right.

Praise God today for justice that gives preference to the poor and lowly. The Prince of Peace is mightily at work, encouraging us to offer shelter to those who are oppressed physically, spiritually, and prayerfully.

By your grace and mercy, O God, you call us to reach out to all people in your love. Embolden us in this calling and lead us in the way of righteousness. Amen.

*J*ob had worn the clothing of righteousness and wrapped himself with the robe and turban of justice. He had been a champion to the needy, with eyes for the blind and feet for the lame.

Where is God in Job's time of need? Job pines for the precious time when in months past God had watched over him and light had shone upon him. Yet even as he shares his plea, God is still actively loving and watching over him.

Job faced a difficult time with many hardships, yet God did not abandon him. The same is true for all of us. We walk through days of darkness where we strain to see any glimmer of light. During those dark days, God is with us as God was with Job, closely loving and watching over him. We all have dark days, but in the darkness, we are safely tucked under God's wing. There, we remain close to God until the dawn breaks.

Gracious God, thank you for being present to us. Even when we can't see or hear you, we know you are here. Amen.

The focus in this passage is usually on the Ethiopian eunuch, but what Philip does is remarkable! An angel of the Lord calls Philip to go, and Philip goes. He is not given a specific destination or task; he asks no questions and does no bartering. We are not told in what form the angel of the Lord takes; we know only that the call came, and Philip recognized it as God's call and obeyed. Philip approaches a chariot, where he encounters the Ethiopian eunuch, who is eager to hear the good news about Jesus.

Would most of us recognize the voice of God? Perhaps the better question is, Do we actively listen for or even expect to hear an angel of the Lord speak to us? Like the eunuch, people are hungry for a word of hope, hungry for a love that comes only from God, hungry to be filled with the amazing news of God's grace!

Where is God leading you to share the good news about Jesus?

Loving God, open our ears and hearts to hear your call, and give us the courage to share the good news of the gospel. Amen.

*T*he early church is struggling to find the middle ground between Christians who adhere to the law and the new Gentile followers. Paul is bridging the gap. Back in Jerusalem, he is eager to share how God is at work among the Gentiles.

The elders praise Paul for his work with the Gentiles; then they immediately ask him to appease those who are still more zealous for the law than the God who freed them from the law. They are so bogged down in the details that they are missing how God is at work through Paul and in Jerusalem. It should be all about the good news of the risen Christ.

There's a lot of discussion today around the question of church membership—what it means and whether it is important. Is it sufficient to agree that Jesus is our Lord and Savior? Or must there be unanimity on everything?

God of grace and love, help us to welcome all who wish to follow you—even those with whom we do not always agree. Amen.

*C*hange is hard. Especially when we are uncertain of what that change means and what difference it will make in our lives. Times of uncertainty can stir up a variety of emotions, often anger or fear, sometimes anticipation or excitement. To these early Christians, it must have seemed as though this relative newcomer, Paul, was changing, or at least challenging, the established rules. The elders attempted a compromise that didn't appease the more legalistic members of the community. Paul doesn't pass their litmus test. It wasn't enough for people to see Paul following the law; his indictment comes because of his work with the Gentiles. The mob thinks that if Paul doesn't do exactly what they do, he must still be against them.

We are creatures of habit. The familiar is easy. Change is hard. While we might not always be overjoyed at the prospect of change, it doesn't mean that change is always bad. Or that the change agent is against the other.

What challenges do you have when you encounter change? What joys have you experienced when changes have occurred in your life?

Help us, God, to assess changes that come before us with some objectivity and to accept change as a part of life. Amen.

$\mathcal{D}$efending himself, his work, and his faith, Paul has reached a point in his testimony where he confesses his call to preach to the Gentiles. It is more than the crowd can stand. Their bloodlust results in Paul's being taken into custody. What makes them so fearful, so threatened by Paul? Is it his radical change from persecutor to missionary? Or is it that his mission is to the Gentiles? It shouldn't be a surprise—Jesus taught and ministered to those who were not Jewish. The disciples were commissioned to make disciples of all nations.

Close your eyes, and place yourself in this scene. Where are you? What are you doing and thinking? How does it make you feel to be there? Now, consider if there's been a time in your life where you felt challenged by someone's call to mission—perhaps with a people with whom you are uncomfortable or whose position on something is different from yours. What feelings does that bring up?

Help us, O God, to see all people as your children and to listen in love as we work through our differences. Amen.

*A*re you convicted enough in your belief of the "hope of the resurrection of the dead" (23:6) to stand up for that belief at the risk of harm? Paul, so sure in his belief, so sure in God, risks his life every time he proclaims the good news to the Gentiles. The fight will not end in Jerusalem; his work is not yet done. As opposition to his ministry mounts, God tells Paul that he will bear witness to his faith in Rome.

There are many times when it seems easier not to speak to our convictions and to play down our faith for fear of offending someone. Perhaps it is because we do not trust God enough. We should be able to share what we believe and how it changes our lives without castigating someone else. If not for God, what will we stand up for?

What does it say about the power of the gospel in our lives if we are afraid to share it?

Gracious God, strengthen and empower us to testify for you with our words and our actions. Amen.

*C*hanged by a powerful conversion, Paul sees the world in a new way. As a devout Jew, a Pharisee, he had always been a zealot for the law, for his faith.

Now Paul has had his eyes opened to a more powerful expression of God's promise—the risen Christ. He has come to see that nothing God does should be a surprise, including raising the dead! He preaches his hope in the promises God has made and no longer preaches hope in keeping the law. He has a new call, a new mission from God to share the good news to the Gentiles.

How many of us have that kind of conviction? Do you live your life in the certainty that God's promises have been and will be fulfilled? Do you burst with the good news of the gospel?

Our lives are the best testimony we have to show God's claim on us and our gratitude for God's amazing gift of grace.

Ineffable God, may what I say and do today reflect your love. Amen.

*P*rior to sharing the story of his conversion with Agrippa, Paul outlines all he did out of his conviction and anger to work against those who followed Jesus. Then things changed.

Paul's conversion story is dramatic. If you grew up in the church, never knowing a time without church, you may not have experienced a dramatic conversion. You may not have questioned your beliefs until you faced something that challenged your faith. Or perhaps some other experiences deepened your faith. Sometimes conversion is about being ready and open to encountering God.

Think back on your experience as a Christian. How did you come to know Jesus? Was there a time when you consciously chose your faith? Did it change your life or how you managed your resources?

If you, like Paul, were called to defend your faith, what would you say?

Holy God, prepare our minds and hearts to recognize opportunities to grow deeper in our faith and our understanding of your work in our lives. Amen.

*P*aul has spoken boldly to friends, enemies, and strangers near and abroad. Now he speaks before King Agrippa, recounting the many trials through which God has brought him. He challenges the king to admit the undeniable: what Moses and the prophets spoke has come to pass with Jesus the Messiah.

We have all been there, in a gathering of disparate people, trying to tread softly and offend no one. Suddenly a slightly quirky person stands and speaks with conviction and clarity. The words are simple and true. How was there ever any doubt? Why had we feared speaking up ourselves?

Paul does not tiptoe. He answers to a higher authority. He speaks unabashedly to the king and his court, proclaiming the reason for the hope that is in him. He describes the life, suffering, death, and resurrection of the Messiah—the One who proclaimed light not only to Jews but also even to despised Gentiles.

Does the gracious authority of the one true God compel you to speak the truth in love?

God, open us to your compelling love. Help us to care enough to speak about what we know to be true. Amen.

*P*aul speaks of his calling as a servant and of the grace and salvation God offers to all the Gentiles. That includes you and me.

Have you ever engaged in a debate over whether true selflessness is possible? Do we ever do things purely for the other person's benefit? I would say yes—but also that we do so through Christ's empowerment.

It is such a basic concept, yet we must relearn it repeatedly: our obedience to God, our good deeds, are a result of God's calling and God's grace through Christ. God's kindness leads us to repentance and good works. As Paul states, it is obedience from faith. Why then do we strive so, with our feeble attempts at selfless kindness, to earn that grace?

God, thank you for reminding us that your grace comes first and that our acts will automatically follow. Give us the faith that leads to obedience. Amen.

*P*aul tells of his gratitude and his prayers for the believers in Rome. He speaks longingly of visiting them and enjoying mutual spiritual encouragement.

In my college days, I treasured every opportunity to get together with another believer. We were intentional about asking each other what God was doing in our lives. We shared Scripture, prayed together, and encouraged each other in the faith. I miss that close fellowship and the difference it made.

A group of friends regularly asked one another three questions: Are you repenting of sin? Are you walking in the light? Are you being broken for others? When we answer these questions honestly, we move beyond surface conversation and into true community.

Paul seemed to avoid small talk. Instead, candor marked his usual conversations. He wanted desperately to visit the Roman believers, to share some spiritual gift to strengthen them.

Looking at Paul's relationships makes me wonder, Do we make the most of our time with other believers?

God, give me eyes to see opportunities today to encourage a friend spiritually and to be encouraged by others. Make us willing to risk the candor that is in our best interest. Amen.

*P*aul longs to see the believers in Rome. He tells how eager he is to share the gospel and describes the power that it brings.

I have often reflected on what it means for the gospel to carry the power to bring someone into a relationship with Christ. This is plainly seen in parts of the world where there is no Scripture translated into the local language.

I remember a summer I spent living with a literacy teacher and a Bible translator. There is nothing like the countenance of a person who is reading the sacred Scriptures for the first time in her or his very own language. In such moments, it is clear that the gospel alone holds all the power needed to open a person's spiritual eyes.

The gospel has phenomenal power in my life and yours. However, to experience this saving power in all its fullness, we immerse ourselves in Scripture. Just a little less web surfing and a little more time in Scripture could take us to a new level.

God, tug me away from distractions today. Help me make the time to ponder Scripture and to experience the saving power it can have in my life. Amen.

*P*aul sets sail from Palestine to Rome, where he is being taken to stand trial. It is fascinating to sift through all the details of this journey, during which those onboard face nonstop challenges. The Scripture passage reads like a long trip gone very wrong and might bring to mind certain past travels that we would like to forget or times of overwhelming crisis.

Bits of information give us a glimpse of how Paul related to those in charge of hauling him to court in Rome. The centurion believed that he could grant Paul temporary release—although perhaps with an escort—to visit with friends while the ship was docked, and he trusted that Paul would return in time for them to launch again. We also see that those in charge respected Paul enough to hear his advice about their travels even though they did not heed his advice.

It seems commonsensical that he built relationships with the authorities even though Paul was not guilty of a crime. Given a similar situation, however, we may not find ourselves quite so willing to practice kindness and civility.

Lord, teach me to behave in every situation in a way that reflects well on you. Amen.

Friday, November 9
Acts 27:13–20

$\mathcal{D}$uring Paul's journey from Palestine to Rome, hopes are dashed as the travelers come upon perilous times. Similarly from time to time we may experience an event so devastating, so completely frightening, that we wonder whether we can make it through. It is in times like these that we may catch a glimpse of the core of a person's character.

We do what we can to avoid these tragedies, but like Paul and his fellow shipmates, sometimes we just have to move forward through the storm. Things are way beyond our control and as an old folk song puts it, there is no way over it, under it, or around it; so we continue through it. Then when just about all hope is gone, we are brought safely to shore.

Hindsight is 20/20, as they say. We may look back and wonder why we did not trust God more fully, whatever the outcome. We may also recall such times when facing our next huge hurdle. Recalling God's past faithfulness is a certain way to boost our hope.

Precious Lord, take my hand. Remind me in those tough times that you hold me in the palm of your hand. Thank you for your unwavering care for me. Amen.

*A*s children, we were warned and advised on many matters, yet we paid little heed. Even when a very wise person reminds us of our past calamities and God's past faithfulness, we are not always quick to hear.

November 10 is the birthday of one of the most faith-full friends I have. She has been known to speak with profound wisdom and to offer advice that comes straight from the heart of God.

In today's passage, Paul speaks wisdom and advice to those with him on the journey to Rome. They face such peril that roles or job titles suddenly seem insignificant. They listen as Paul tells them of a visit he had with "an angel of the God to whom I belong and whom I worship" (v. 23) and urges them to have courage.

As the sailors let down the lifeboat and attempt to jump ship, Paul warns his military escorts that they will be saved only if they stay onboard. They cut off the ropes to their earthly lifeboat and wait for God alone to deliver them.

Who are the wise people in your life? Whose advice do you always seek when you are faced with a dilemma or an important decision? Give thanks for that wise person.

Heavenly captain, thank you for your unchanging presence that brings us to safety when we allow ourselves to cut loose the ropes. Amen.

The movie *The Perfect Storm* evokes the horrors of being on a boat in a terrible storm. The crew's emotional and physical trials as they try to save their vessel and themselves leave the viewer exhausted. This movie came to mind when reading Luke's detailed account of a long-ago shipwreck.

A prisoner aboard a ship sailing for Rome, Paul surely experienced heart-stopping fear when his ship ran into a fierce storm. Moreover, considering that the storm came soon after an attack by an angry mob in Jerusalem, Paul could be forgiven for wondering just how much more he could endure!

Paul maintains a presence in the midst of the chaos that belies what is happening. He offers direction and leadership that is necessary in the frightening moments. He sounds a voice of certain hope in the midst of the frantic struggle for survival. Despite what surely must have seemed overwhelming and uncertain, Paul is certain of God's care, God's concern, and God's plans.

In what frightening places do you find yourself today? How can God's trustworthiness lead you safely to shore?

God of all storms, help us to trust in your guiding love. Amen.

$\mathcal{D}$rive on any street in America, read the bumper stickers on the cars you see, and you know something about the inhabitants of the vehicle: "My other car is a broom." "Corporations are not people." "Don't hate; educate." "Spread your work ethic, not your wealth." We have a need to share something of ourselves—to make ourselves known—and sometimes a bumper sticker is just the right tool!

Ezekiel speaks God's words of anger and judgment in some of the strangest ways recorded in Scripture. He tells the Israelites that God wants to be known and to make a home in their midst. God wants the Israelite leaders to help make God known as well by demonstrating God's love and care to God's people.

Do your actions help make God known to those around you? Jesus said we are to feed the hungry, clothe the naked, and love one another. As we serve God by serving others, we point the way to a God who loves us and wants to be in a relationship with us.

God of love, may our lives of service make your love known to others. Amen.

*I*n the great green room, there was a telephone and a red balloon." When I first read this sentence from the classic *Goodnight Moon* to my granddaughter, she looked puzzled. "Where's the telephone?" she asked. The picture of the rotary telephone was unrecognizable to her, having known only a world of cell phones.

Our understanding of shepherds is equally limited, so we can be grateful for Ezekiel's beautiful images of God's work as a shepherd caring for God's flock. This picture comes as the temple has been destroyed and the Israelites are reaping the consequences of their failure to keep covenant with God.

Instead of saying, "I told you so," God searches for and rescues us from our destructive tendencies. God is concerned about our physical needs and offers healing and strength for life. God wants all of us to live together justly and in peace.

Ezekiel's words offer hope and comfort to a people who are scattered, grieving, and divided. How do these words offer comfort to you when you experience division, sorrow, and need?

Gracious God, we are grateful that we can never be out of the reach of your love. Amen.

Over the last forty years, the size of the average home increased in size by more than 55 percent although family size shrank. The typical home has more TVs than people. A blueberry muffin at a popular restaurant is 233 percent bigger than USDA recommendations. We are people of privilege in a world in which more than a billion people live in poverty.

God has some strong words for people whose power and privilege create divided communities; it can be uncomfortable to read these verses. But God is clear. Our use of God's good gifts must not be enjoyed at the expense of the weakest and least respected in our communities. God expects us to live in such a way that our actions and choices enhance the possibility of life for all.

How do we evaluate our desires and needs in light of the needs in our communities? The answer to that question can take a variety of forms, but Ezekiel tells us that our response to that question matters to God.

God of grace, forgive us for the ways in which we live selfishly in your world. Amen.

Christmas on Exeter Street tells of a family whose doorbell rings many times on Christmas Eve, revealing a new set of faces and new requests each time. One of the last illustrations shows a motley assortment of strangers and friends sleeping in every possible nook and cranny of the house. Sometimes the bed is a mantle, or a kitchen sink, or a china cupboard. The inscription in the front of the book simply reads, "Romans 12:13." Practice hospitality.

I love the connection between Christmas and Paul's vision of the new life we have in Christ. This new life takes shape in a community; practicing hospitality is a hallmark of how we are to relate to one another. When we share bread and wine around the Lord's Table, we practice Christ's radical hospitality that says all are welcome, all are served and fed, and no one is a stranger.

How can we best share that hospitality in our churches, in our homes, and in our hearts? Where are the strangers in your world who need to know and experience the welcome of the Christian community?

Loving God, open our hearts and our communities to those we see as strangers. Amen.

*R*ecently the good cooks in my husband's family compiled
a cookbook of old recipes they had loved as children and
new ones they now use. While preparing these recipes, I
recall family stories and good times spent around the table.
The cookbook gives practical instructions for meals and bears
testimony to a family's life together.

Approaching the end of his ministry, Paul sends Timothy a
kind of recipe book. He has written many letters of profound
theology; this one is personal and practical. He leaves a record
of his life in service to God and a recipe for this life: "Watch
your words. Avoid being caught up in senseless controversies.
Be kind." In following this recipe for a disciplined life of love,
Timothy will bear testimony to God's work in the church.

Our faith is not determined by how well we follow a set of
rules. However, how we live our lives enables God to use us
more effectively in God's work of bringing good news to the
world. Do our lives bear testimony to God's claim on us? Do
they reflect our readiness for God to use us?

*Use me, Lord; use even me. Just as Thou wilt, and when, and where.
Amen.*

*I*n a recent conversation, a minister shared his feelings about his last month in his church after he had accepted a new call. He described his life as having one foot in the right-now of his current work and another foot in the not-yet of his new congregation as he prepared to move.

Facing persecution, the Thessalonian church was thinking about Christ's return and their future. Paul responds by telling them not to worry. Their future and present are in God's hands. Therefore, they are to live in the light of that hope.

Paul's list of attributes of faithful living can seem overwhelming. Instead of criticizing the morning's sermon at lunch, we're called to appreciate our leaders. We are to exercise patience when our patience is at an end. We're called to do good to all even when we're not able to be considerate to those we love the most.

Do good to all? It seems impossible, given our sinfulness. However, we trust God, whose kingdom is greater than our weakness and who can use our smallest acts of faithfulness to make it known.

God of our past, present, and future, thank you for the vocation of faithful living to which you call us. Amen.

$\mathcal{M}$y friend Josh is a seminary student who served for a year as a hospital chaplain. He told me of a visit he made to a hospitalized prison inmate who wore handcuffs and had a guard at his door. During their visit, they never discussed the man's reason for imprisonment. Instead, Josh discovered that the sick man had been a gardener and asked his advice on his mother's pepper-growing efforts. "No one's asked me a question like that in fifteen years," the man responded with tears in his eyes. Josh said that it felt like holy ground.

Given what we know about Paul, we might have expected him to try to establish a new church on Malta. Luke tells us that Paul healed the sick—a ministry so important that Christ commanded his disciples to join him in it.

Praying for the sick is something we do easily. However, do we really see ourselves as participating in healing? God calls us to serve the sick, and in our prayers, our visits, our casseroles, our touch, we may be a means by which we stand together on holy ground in God's presence where healing takes place.

Great healer, make your presence known to all in need of wholeness. Amen.

$\mathcal{G}$o, tell it on the mountain." "Tell out, my soul, the greatness of God's name." "Tell me the stories of Jesus." Some of my favorite hymns describe the joy in telling and being told the story of God's presence in the world.

Moses doesn't seem to find joy in telling the Israelites. They aren't listening! God doesn't tell Moses that God will find someone more eloquent or persuasive. God just tells Moses to talk to someone else. Already discouraged because his people don't listen, Moses wants God to find someone else to do the talking.

We sometimes want God to find someone else. Someone else to teach our youth class. Someone else to speak truth to power. Someone else to confront the pain and injustice and hurt in this world and talk of God's plan for peace.

Fortunately, who listens isn't up to us. It is up to God. God only asks us to be responsible for telling what we have known and experienced through God's grace and know that God can use our inadequate words for God's loving purposes.

God, may we joyfully tell the story of your gracious love to the world. Amen.

*A*n Internet discussion board for parents recently dealt with how you keep a strong relationship with your children as they go through adolescence. Avoiding saying "I told you so" seemed to be the key for many of these parents in maintaining some kind of familiar equilibrium during these trying years.

My sympathies lie with the Israelites here. Who among us hasn't felt the guilt associated with knowing that we didn't listen to good advice and made a mess of things? Who among us hasn't recognized that we failed to heed the good words that even God gives us that demand our response? It is hard to stand up to the anger or anguish with which those words are delivered when we know we are wrong.

It is then that we turn to grace, to the promise that God will walk with us despite our failings. The Israelites knew that love despite how often they failed to keep covenant with God. We know it as well, and the sure and certain knowledge that God loves us despite our failure to heed God's living word can help to keep our ears open for what God has to say to us next.

God of mercy, forgive us when we fail to hear and heed your commandments. Amen.

When we were younger, my siblings and I had to memorize Scripture on Sunday afternoons. I later asked my parents how they had determined what we would learn. My mother recounted being influenced early in her parenting life by hearing of Russian children at camp when Hitler invaded Russia who were unable to return home. A schoolteacher got the children to safety, but there is no record that these families were ever reunited. What, my parents wondered, would they want to leave with us as guidance if we had to live life without them?

Moses might be considering the same questions as he prepares to send the Israelites into the promised land without him. They will face cultures and practices that will tempt them from their calling as God's covenant people. What they know and have experienced will be crucial to preserving their identity as God's own as they move into their new land.

If our knowledge and experience are reflected in the way we live our lives, what are we teaching others about God? What have you been taught or observed in other faithful people that has shaped your life of faith?

By what we learn and share, O God, help us make your word known fully. Amen.

Battle Hymn of the Tiger Mother recounts author Amy Chau's efforts to raise her children in "the Chinese way." This parenting style includes not allowing her children to attend sleepovers, berating them for anything less than an A, and throwing handmade birthday cards back if she felt they were inferior work. The response has been a boisterous conversation coalescing around Chinese strictness and Western permissiveness. It is really a debate about discipline. To what end do we discipline our children?

Moses refers to discipline. His sermon is based on the Second Commandment: God first; God alone. Discipline for Moses includes remembering God's mighty acts with thanksgiving and obeying the commandments as a guide to daily life.

Discipline and *disciple* are related words. God's discipline is not harsh nor is it punishment. God calls us to become disciples not by criticizing or devaluing us but by offering the example of Christ. God shapes us still.

God of love, we are grateful for our experience of your loving discipline as we seek to follow you alone. Amen.

The whole book of Deuteronomy is a constant call to faithfulness and obedient discipleship. Obedience should be a natural response to God's active presence in our lives: deliverance from bondage, guidance and safety through life, and a promised homeland. God wants to be in relationship with the Israelites, and God wants to be in relationship with us.

Love the Lord your God in order that you might live. It is an invitation to the Israelites and to us to follow a God who offers a different kind of life. God does not leave us alone as we live into that life. God made a home with the people of Israel; God makes a home in our world. We have been given the church to support and encourage us in our walk of faith. We have been given a vocation—to serve God. Moreover, we have been given the living Word that we meet each time we share the sacrament of bread and wine together. God speaks a present word of grace, forgiveness, and hope.

Ever-present God, may your love guide us in the way of life. Amen.

*W*e turn on a radio program driving to work or keep an ear open to commentators on the evening news. We attend committee meetings and make telephone calls. We attend a lecture, or just listen to a friend or family member share his or her day. We hear many words each day.

Paul traveled the Mediterranean world speaking to those who needed and wanted to hear his encouragement and teaching. Now his situation has changed; he is a house prisoner in Rome. He must wait for people to come to him. However, when they come, he is ready to keep sharing.

We may never have world leaders or enthusiastic crowds sitting at our feet to hear us speak, but our homes can be places where we share words of compassion and care. The sales clerks with whom we converse can hear words of appreciation. The colleague whose opinion is very different from ours can hear words of respect. The depressed friend can hear words of encouragement and hope. Is what people hear from you a reflection of Christ's love and claim on you?

Lord, in speaking and listening, may we be attuned to your living word. Amen.

*I*f there is one thing you can say about the apostle Paul, it is that he never pulled punches with anyone. It is clear where he stood on matters of faith. Among Paul's many visitors during his house arrest in Rome, only some believed his message about Jesus and the law of Moses, while more than most walked away arguing among themselves and not believing the message.

Paul reminds us that we are called to proclaim the good news of the gospel even in the face of those who may scoff at us. We are called to live a life that follows Christ's example. Doing so may ultimately teach more than words can convey, even when others have "shut their eyes" and their "hearts have grown dull" (v. 27).

During Paul's two years of house arrest, he welcomed all and continued to proclaim the kingdom of God and teach about Jesus with boldness and without hindrance.

God, we are not called to be timid Christians; we are called to proclaim your love bravely and without hesitation. Give us the courage to live your love out loud every day. Amen.

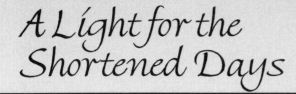

A Light for the Shortened Days

*I*f you're happy and you know it, clap your hands. If you're happy and you know it, clap your hands. . . ." You can probably sing the rest of this song. You may have learned this song as a child or taught this song to a young child.

This psalm conveys the joy of forgiveness and, according to scholars, was likely used as a tool of instruction in the temple. It guided worshipers in the understanding of the release found in confession, the power of grace received, and the happiness experienced from forgiveness.

There is blessed relief when we stop covering up our sins and confess them to God and one another. The psalmist says that there are "glad cries of deliverance" (v. 7) when God's forgiveness is received—perhaps even the kind of glad cries that might lead the forgiven one to clap his or her hands in happiness.

God of Grace, you grant us peace when we confess our transgressions. Happy are we who learn this lesson well, for we shall clap our hands with joy. Amen.

$\mathcal{R}$emember how happy you were in grade school when you were chosen to be on a team? Remember how especially happy you were to not be the last one chosen?

Psalm 33:8–12 says people will find happiness only if they fear the Lord. The psalmist tells us nations will find happiness when they seek the counsel of the Lord rather than depending on their plans and initiatives.

The Hebrew people understood themselves as God's heritage. As Christians, we believe that by adoption through our redemption in Jesus Christ, we too are chosen as God's heritage.

To embrace the truth that God does the choosing and not we is actually empowering. Time does not have to be wasted on worrying about who's in and who's out. Understanding and accepting that God is God and that we are not are blessings that free us to live grateful lives as ones grafted into God's family.

Sovereign Lord of all, you are indeed an awesome God. We know that your wisdom stands forever. We are reminded to seek your counsel in all we do and to be grateful that we are grafted into your household, chosen as your heritage. Amen.

I recently lost my job and had to reassess what defines my identity. Losing sight of our true selves can happen in a variety of ways—the departure of a loved one, children growing up and moving away, retirement, or a physical impairment. The question then becomes, "In spite of all the change, is there something greater that truly defines who I am?"

Paul's first letter to the church in Corinth begins with an affirmation of the identity of the faithful people: "I give thanks to my God always for you because of the grace of God that has been given you in Christ Jesus. . . . God is faithful; by him you were called into the fellowship of his son, Jesus Christ our Lord" (vv. 4, 9).

When tough times shake us to our core and our very identity is threatened, it is a blessing to have the reassurance of who we are as believers in Jesus Christ, and, more importantly, to know whose we are. We are defined by God's grace.

God of grace and God of glory, through Jesus Christ, we have been blessed with the assurance that we are yours. We can say with unshakable confidence, "I am a child of God." Because of your faithful love, we shall always know who we are and whose we are. Amen.

*K*nowledge is power. People often hold on to perceived power by withholding knowledge from others. Keeping information to oneself puts one in a position of power over another. In today's text, we see how God turns this concept upside down.

As Daniel prays, he acknowledges that wisdom and power belong to God alone. He affirms that God shares this power by giving wisdom to the wise and knowledge to those who have understanding. At the close of the prayer, Daniel gives thanks to God: "for you have given me wisdom and power . . ." (v. 23).

God chooses to empower us with knowledge and wisdom. Are we wise enough to receive the gift? To do so, we must first humbly acknowledge the source of all wisdom and power— God. Then we must be open to discerning God's message. Finally, we need to give God all the glory for the knowledge we have discerned.

We are blessed when we receive God's gift of wisdom and power, when we humbly share it with others, and when we give God the glory.

God of wisdom and power, give us the wisdom to discern your message, the strength of character to share it with others, and the humility to give you all honor and glory. Amen.

To the church in Colossae, Paul was known only by reputation. They had heard and accepted the truth of the gospel through the work of Epaphras, a disciple of Paul.

Using the triadic formula of faith, love, and hope in his letter to the Colossians, Paul praised this band of believers for their acceptance of the gospel. He lauded the way that they embraced the truth of the good news. Paul encouraged the people with a vision of how their faith would bear fruit throughout the whole world.

If ever there was a simple answer to the question of how we Christians should live, this would be it—have faith in Jesus Christ; share that faith and Christ's love with others, and live in the hope that the truth of the gospel will bear fruit throughout the world.

The word of truth blesses us when we hear it preached, read, or sung. The word of truth is a blessing when we work to live faithful lives abounding in love and hope.

God of truth, may we embrace the gospel and share it with all whom we meet, and may the word of truth bear fruit forever. Amen.

*F*or someone who was rendered mute for nigh on nine months, Zechariah's first words after regaining his voice were powerful ones. Zechariah's Song is not only a prophecy concerning the future of his newborn son John, but it is also a prophecy about the coming of a mighty savior.

Salvation and redemption are themes woven throughout Zechariah's prophecy. His message proclaims that God redeems the people, raises up a mighty savior, remembers the holy covenant, rescues from enemies, brings salvation to the people, and forgives sins. To those who heard this prophecy in that day and time, those who suffered oppression and political upheaval, these welcome words foretold a bright future.

These words also sound pretty good to us today. As we look around the world and in our own backyards, we see the need for God's redemption every day. We worry over the future of this earth we call home. There is a sense that evil continues to gain the upper hand. Hear the good news—through Jesus Christ, we have been redeemed!

God of mercy, your promise is true, and your covenant, sure. You have looked favorably upon us. Blessed be the Lord, for redemption is ours. Amen.

*R*ead this passage aloud—that's really the only way to understand it. Imagine trying to read it in one breath, with your voice gradually growing in intensity and joy, a crescendo of glorious praise.

These introductory words of the letter to the Ephesians were written as one long sentence in the Greek! Modern translations try to chop this passage up into more manageable prose, but it's intended to be a soaring hymn, a resounding doxology.

How else to express the boundless blessings, the limitless love of God offered to us in Christ Jesus? By the amazing grace of God, we have been chosen for redemption in Christ and claimed as beloved children. This took place before the dawning of creation. Now, baptized into Christ and sealed by the Holy Spirit, we are a part of God's promise and plan for the fulfillment of all things. Amazing. No wonder the writer is breathless with praise!

Let your life, all your words and actions, bear witness to this "run-on sentence of redemption"—God's saving story, stretching from the foundation of the world to the coming of a new creation.

"Let everything that has breath praise the LORD! Hallelujah!"
(Psalm 150:6). Amen.

I lived next to a "waste place" in England for several years, a vacant lot with an open basement where a home once stood. This horrible hole symbolized all that was wrong with my life: I felt in exile in a place where I didn't always understand the local dialect, had to walk several miles to buy food, and was in shock every time I looked at the price of eggs or milk. The factory next door spewed sawdust and noise.

But my life changed for the better. My husband and I flew back to the United States and lived in a quiet neighborhood. We could afford car payments and groceries. Family was near, and the neighbors were kind.

Isaiah spoke encouragement to a people who suffered in exile, who inhabited desolate places. God will transform you and bring comfort for your wretchedness, and joy, not pain. This is sure; salvation will come.

Looking back, my small exile gave me an appreciation of the misery others endure due to poverty and loneliness. I also learned deep dependency on God. We know that a nation can be reduced to rubble and despair. We also know deliverance will come, for God's salvation goes out, working transformation that surpasses human dreams.

Eternal God, have mercy on all who despair. Comfort them, and lead them out of waste places into the garden of your presence; through Christ our Lord. Amen.

*O*ne spring I planted several blueberry bushes. The first year, I harvested five berries. The next year, twenty, and not all at the same time. I realized that someone else, years later, would come to the bushes and fill his or her bowl. Another friend told me of moving to a new house and discovering eight-foot-high blueberry bushes in the backyard. He reaped where another sowed.

We plant trees, but someone else may sit in their shade. We plant fruit trees, but someone else might pluck the apples. We invest toward the future for the sake of others.

We do not see the meaning of our lives as God sees. We may feel like small twigs barren of fruit. Day by day, we may wonder about the purpose of our lives. Sometimes nothing seems to be happening, but God made us with purpose. We cannot see the ripple effects of our kindness and charity, our words and gestures, our work, or our children and the generations that follow. We belong wholly to God. God knows the full dimensions of our lives and will witness the fruition and harvest.

Blessed God, you made me to abide in you and bear much fruit. Thank you for blessing my efforts a hundredfold through the power of Christ our Lord. Amen.

*W*e trudge a well-worn path to Bethlehem to do business and encounter the usual frustrations. We have forgotten our toothbrushes, find the hotel booked, and end up out back with the cows. Rotten food, too much noise.

Along the way are people: crying people, hungry people, shushed children, extravagant women, outcasts; tax collector up a tree; gluttons, fearful people, widow on your knees, Lazarus on a slab. Class clown, resident geek, mechanic extraordinaire, lawyer, teacher, factory worker, CEO, mayor, snowplow driver.

Christ comes to each one seeking room to be born. Give him the luxury suite, the economy room near the stairs with bad plumbing or stick him out back altogether while you think it over: if you don't turn Jesus away, he lodges with you.

Welcome Christ, and be blessed.

Lord Jesus Christ, come to my heart; stay with me; bless me and give me joy; through the power of your Holy Spirit. Amen.

$\mathcal{G}$od repairs the breach. Where there is enmity, God promises restoration. The Bible is filled with stories that have surprise endings: older people have babies, reviving hope for the future; siblings reconcile after years of hostility; and foreigners like Ruth join the family of God, pledging to worship the God of Abraham and Sarah.

Paul says that it's a mystery, God's intention to bring together Jews and Gentiles. But is it really? God's been doing that kind of work for a long time.

Maybe it's a mystery because we forget. We seem to be more committed to the dividing walls of hostility than we'd care to admit. Walls help us define who's in and out and give a sense of security.

God's not about a safe, easy security; God calls us to an adventure, a risky endeavor, a truly open table with a place for everyone. Check your table—is there a place for everyone? Whom do you exclude?

Compassionate God, bring my prejudices to light, that I may repent of them, be forgiven, and healed; through Christ my Lord. Amen.

*H*ave you ever had someone pray for you—for you specifically, someone who knows you well, someone you respect and care for?

Paul prays for a group of people he cares for deeply. This prayer is not limited just to them. In these words, there is a prayer for all who follow Jesus Christ. That means a prayer for you.

Paul prays that God may grant them (and us) inner strength from the Holy Spirit. He asks Jesus Christ to dwell with us in such a way that we are ever aware of his presence, and through us, always present in and for the world. And that they (and we!) will understand the cosmic extent of God's work, threaded through with the love of Jesus Christ that reaches beyond comprehension.

What a prayer! A prayer for every follower of Jesus Christ—in Paul's day, in ours, in the future. Let the power of that prayer carry you this day; let it shape how you look at and respond to the world around you.

God, grant us your strength, that our lives and words will testify to Jesus' presence and power in and for the world. Amen.

347

One night I dreamed I was in the ocean as a large wave approached. I was dangerously near rocks in the powerful, surging water. I ducked under the surface so the huge wave would wash over me. Crouched in front of a rock, I found a nail that had fixed Christ to the cross. At that instant, the huge wave froze, suspended. I was saved by taking refuge in Christ.

The death of Christ on the cross and his resurrection three days later is our surety. God, who raised Jesus from death, will surely look after those adopted as children in the covenant of baptism.

In baptism, we take hold of God's promise of new life, are submerged in the waters, and are given birth in Christ. He becomes the touchstone of our hearts, the anchor of our souls, our refuge.

We can seize the good news as our hope and look forward to fruitfulness and security: we are God's beloved children forever. The nails of the cross are symbols of salvation, our safety in Christ.

Faithful God, you protect all who take refuge in you. Keep me close to you all my days so that, secure in your love, I may serve you with boldness and joy through Christ our Lord. Amen.

*W*hat time is it?

There is the past: "You were dead through the trespasses and sins in which you once lived . . ." (Ephesians 2:1). A past at odds with God and God's purposes.

Or not, for God sees differently: "But God, who is rich in mercy, out of the great love with which he loved us even when we were dead through our trespasses . . ." (2:4). We look back and see brokenness. God looks back and sees the repair of our brokenness, the forgiveness of our sin.

There is the future. "God . . . made us alive together with Christ . . . and raised us up with him and seated us with him in the heavenly places in Christ Jesus" (2:5–6).

There is the present: "For we are what he has made us, created in Christ Jesus for good works, which God prepared beforehand to be our way of life" (2:10).

What time is it in your life today? Time to look back? To look ahead? To see in the present the good works God has prepared for you, to be your way of life?

Most High God, help us see the good works you have prepared for us. Give us courage to venture into the future you have promised. Amen.

*N*o more day and night. Summer and winter passing away. The land leveled, and the city of God towering above it all. A river of living water flowing in two directions, from the center of the city to the ends of the earth. What in the world is going on here?

Well, nothing in the world. These are scenes from the world to come, God's new creation. Zechariah offers images that remind us of the first and last chapters of the Bible: the creation of day and night in Genesis 1; and the vision of the city of God in Revelation 22, where there is endless light and a river flowing from God's throne. From top to bottom, from beginning to end, God is making all things new.

As we watch and wait for signs of God's coming realm, we are called to proclaim the name of the Lord to all the earth: The Lord is our God, the Lord alone!

"I am the Alpha and Omega, the beginning and the end. To the thirsty, I will give water as a gift from the spring of the water of life" (Revelation 21:6).

*P*aul entreats the Philippians to "live your life in a manner worthy of the gospel of Christ" (v. 27). The gospel cannot remain merely in our thoughts or even in our prayers; it must be manifested in our life.

What does it mean to live a life worthy of the gospel that includes striving, struggling, confrontations, and suffering for Christ? We are more familiar and comfortable with Paul at the end of Philippians where he writes to live joyfully in the Lord: "Rejoice in the Lord always; again I will say, Rejoice" (4:4). Joy is part of the spectrum of living out the gospel. There is no true joy in gospel life without suffering for Christ. Joy and suffering are not mutually exclusive.

Paul is talking about a corporate action in which we bear one another's suffering, "striving side by side with one mind for the faith of the gospel" (v. 27). It entails a community that does not avoid or hide suffering, one that communicates and shares the suffering of its members together. How can we take small steps toward becoming such a transparent community that will live out life in a manner worthy of the gospel of Christ?

Gracious Savior, bind us together in such a way that we bear one another's burdens and sorrows. To God's glory. Amen.

I love to watch a TV show where someone at wit's end invites a crew inside their cluttered home for a makeover. Eyebrows arch as the host surveys clothes strewn over the floor, boxes piled high in bedrooms, trash and treasures mingled on carpets. The homeowners do emergency triage and sell excess stuff in a yard sale. The decorators transform ugly rooms to stunning ones. Once the packrats see their new digs, they have no desire to return to messy quarters.

Faithful people uproot themselves from old mind-sets to see what new thing God desires to do through them. They see evidence piled up in Scripture—new wineskins, new creatures, new life beyond death—and are persuaded to detach themselves from the familiar to welcome God's designs.

I have never heard a spiritual person say, "I was better off before I knew God's love." No one who tastes God's kindness desires to retreat from it and return to a restless heart.

Christ calls us to a new way.

Merciful God, you see when I fear change, but you have good things in store for me. Help me to grasp your hand that I may receive newness of life; through Christ my Savior. Amen.

$\mathcal{M}$any of us may think of God's laws as mandatory obligations that we need to keep in order to be accepted by God. We may even think that God's laws are in opposition to God's grace in Christ. Instead, try to believe that God's law is an expression of God's grace.

Before the Ten Commandments are articulated in this chapter, verse 2 clearly identifies the kind of God who is giving these laws to the Israelites: "I am the Lord your God, who brought you out of the land of Egypt, out of the house of slavery."

The law is not given to the Israelites as a requirement for the exodus. God did not say, "If you obey these commandments, I will rescue you from slavery." God had already brought the Israelites out of Egypt and gave the commandments as a gift to God's people as a guide to help them live faithfully to the God who has already saved them.

Let us then gladly and thankfully worship only this God.

O God, we would worship you with gladness and come into your presence with singing. Amen.

I can almost see Paul pointing to different people in the
Corinthian congregation as he speaks: "You have the gift of
wisdom, and you have the gift of knowledge; you have the gift
of prophecy, and you have the gift of discernment." The point
Paul is making is this: we each have different gifts and different
roles in the body of Christ (the church). We are many, yet we
are one. The mysterious way that many are made one is by the
power of the one Spirit, one Lord, and one God, who gives us
talents and skills and calls us into service.

It's tempting when we read this list of spiritual gifts to try
to identify our specific gifts. If we don't fit into one of these
categories, we may think that we have less to offer, but the list
should not be taken as exhaustive or complete.

The body of Christ needs all of us—all of our gifts. The same
God who gathers us also uses those gifts "for the common
good." The church, the body of Christ, has many members and
needs them all.

*Holy God, embrace us with manifold grace that we might serve
one another with the gifts each of us has received. Amen.*

There was a socially awkward, quiet little boy, about nine years old. His mother and father were divorced, his father hardly ever saw him. His foster grandmother was concerned for his well-being and brought him to talk to her pastor every Monday for an hour. Gradually "Robert" began to talk, smile, and show confidence.

I think that Robert will grow up with gratitude for his grandmother, who helped him open up to others. I think she influenced him to grow into a kind and sensitive person. I think he'll remember the man who talked with him and made him feel at home in his skin. Robert learned kindness from the kind, compassion from the compassionate. Everyone around him will feel the ripples from those gentle Monday afternoon conversations.

Paul's counsel calls us to receive every Robert with warmth, compassion, and encouragement. Do our smiles say, "I accept you"? An arm around the shoulder, a comment whispered in the ear, can mark a providential fork in the road, a turn toward trust and joy.

God, you have shown me great kindness. May I be a loving influence on others, through the grace of Christ our Lord. Amen.

Several years ago, I taught classes in ministry to seventeen men at Sing Sing Correctional Facility, a maximum security prison in Ossining, New York. The days I went to the prison involved careful wardrobe choices, knowing that I would pass through humbling searches and scans. The day would involve my walking both inside and outside, hoping to catch the prison shuttle bus but prepared to walk if an escort could be found for the civilian volunteer. I felt like a suspect and not particularly welcome.

When I arrived at the classroom, I found men eager to learn although many would never see the light of freedom. They were already living exemplary lives of service within the prison system and counted it a gift to learn to exercise their gifts of ministry.

Paul speaks in the voice of the prisoner but as one who has not given up the hope that his life would matter, that his influence would make a difference. Many of the men I was teaching would exercise the gifts of ministry in a prison for the rest of their lives. What gifts do we have for ministry? What is the unique gift of our call, and are we committed to using these gifts in all of the circumstances life may hold for us?

God, awaken the Spirit's gifts within us that we may serve you faithfully and well. Amen.

*G*od my shelter,
  it was your will to bring me very low
  and dwell with me there.

After many months,
  you showed me the true nature
  of my terrible night:
  your blessèd wing
  arched over me,
  blotting out the light.

You will awaken me
  when it is dawn,
  when your wing
  stirs.

*God, thank you for your loving presence. I take refuge in your
strength and wisdom; through Christ my Savior. Amen.*

*M*y sixth-grade homeroom teacher was far from typical. His six-foot-five lanky body, carried by high-top shoes, swayed as he traveled the halls and ducked through doorways. If his basketball career taught him anything, it was how to coach. We learned about more than the books could teach us that year from Mr. Dermott; we learned about life. He taught us history and how to be history makers; about fair play and care for the outcast. More than a teacher, he was our coach, our mentor, and our leader.

Ephesians 4:21–22 serves as a reminder that those formed in Christ that are lost are taught a better way. Who has taught you and formed you? In what ways are you continuing to learn and grow? How could you "be renewed in the spirit" (v. 23) today and in the days to come?

Teacher and renewer of our faith, forgive us for what we have done or left undone that goes not glorify you. Form us and reform us in your image that we might more clearly reflect your image to the world. Amen.

*M*y late husband was a pastor of another denomination. After he died, I went to a church in a nearby city and sat alone in a pew. I went another Sunday and sat alone again. This continued nearly two years when finally someone asked me to sit with her. I was overjoyed but never saw her again. Only two people regularly greeted me. They sat in the chancel.

There were other difficulties with this church: wherever I sat, people were noisy. One elder wrote notes during worship, rustling papers the whole time. Finally, I left. A hospital chaplain confided that it was the most spiritually troubled church in town. I then focused on supply preaching, and people were always glad to see me.

As I write this, I get up from my desk to put some laundry in the dryer. It occurs to me that you might ask, "Why didn't you invite someone to sit with you?" At the time, I was hurting and did not want to risk rejection. I know, however, that being a friend of God means befriending others and that faith needs to be expressed in action, not simply in thoughts and intentions. God sent Jesus as the Word in flesh, not in a dream.

How will you live faith today?

Merciful God, in Jesus you have shown me what love requires. Help me to minister to the sick, feed the hungry, aid the homeless, and welcome strangers; in Jesus' name. Amen.

*H*ow can we tell if someone is responsible and trustworthy? It can be hard to know. A couple opened a restaurant and served savory soups, great bread, and mouth-watering baked goods. After several years, they had to close their business because an employee embezzled much of the profit.

Those who betray trust trigger upheavals in the lives of those affected. If we are betrayed, we tend to monitor everyone for evidence of further deceit. Being a lie detector is exhausting. Trust allows us to lower our defenses and be ourselves; it is the foundation of thriving, loving relationships.

You are a soul whom God has planted. Grow your roots deep in the depth of God, and without question you will bear good fruit. Blessing will ripple out from you in a widening circle whose unseen center is God. One trusting soul can feed thousands.

God, blessed are those who trust in you: you lead them from strength to strength. No good thing do you withhold from them. You give me strength, and my heart is filled with joy. I rest in the shadow of your wings; I make your love my home and sing your praise forever through Christ, my light, my life, my way. Amen.
(Based on Psalm 84)

*A*nd there, ahead of them, went the star that they had seen at its rising, until it stopped over the place where the child was" (v. 9).

One day I was invited on a country outing to visit the home of composer Edward Elgar. My friend pulled the car to a stop at an intersection and ignored the sign giving directions to our destination. "Oh, well," I thought. I didn't know her well enough to comment. We arrived at the Elgar home an hour and a half later. I loved seeing the beautiful English countryside, but I don't want to be lost or clueless on a regular basis.

We want our GPS, computer directions, or map; we complain if they misdirect us by one block. We want to be in the driver's seat with both hands on the steering wheel. Faith, however, means letting go so that God can drive. This is why it is so difficult.

With God, there is risk. As Jesus said to Peter, "When you grow old . . . someone else will . . . take you where you do not wish to go" (John 21:18). We cannot grow without risk, and we cannot become a blessing to others without growth. No one ever said that formation in Christ was comfortable. But new life is worth it. Looking back, do you think the magi would have said, "No, I'm not going. I don't want to risk the wrath of Herod"? Would you? I didn't think so.

God, help me to journey with you in trust, that my life may be a blessing to others; through Jesus Christ. Amen.

_T_he Word became flesh and lived among us" (v. 14).

On my study wall is a Victorian picture of a girl praying. A shaft of gold light extends from the girl's eyes toward heaven and from God to the child. She and God are present to each other. When we seek the Lord, our gaze meets that of the divine.

Christians of the past reflected on Scripture, the natural world, and their experience. This spiritual practice, called "meditation," gradually led them to a deeper openness to God.

Remember, re-member (hyphen intentional)—that is, make present in your awareness—Jesus' incarnation, his en-flesh-ment. He was born in Bethlehem; he has been born in our hearts. Let the mystery of holy beginnings bring you to wonder. Look at Jesus. He gazes on you: you are present to each other. Thank God!

Covenant God, you are faithful forever. You are my God; I am your child. Help me to remember so that my heart may leap for joy; in Jesus' name. Amen.

*C*andles glowed on the Communion Table as Ron began to preach. After a few minutes, I noticed a light softly glowing but dismissed it. Later that evening as I prayed, the light returned. I felt the presence of the Compassionate One, full of utter kindness and happiness, and was at peace. Then God departed; I was by myself once more.

Jesus is the Light of God clothed in flesh, and Mary is the one chosen to give him birth. We would do well to remember her encounter with the angel of God more than once a year. She has purity of heart and complete inner freedom to accept God without hesitation.

Some of us may ponder God all our lives without satisfying answers. Mary the mother of Jesus lived as a child of the light; the angel answered her questions, perhaps not to her liking or according to her expectations. But because she trusted God, she followed the question, "How can this be?" with "Here am I, the servant of the Lord; let it be with me according to your word."

May we say to God, "Here I am," and "Let it be." God will come to light.

God Most High, give me an open heart to bear Christ to the world; through your Holy Spirit. Amen.

*M*y mother used the word *no* the way others used *hmm*—as a transition from one phrase to another. I felt squashed after hearing no for many years. I longed to hear her say yes with luminous eyes and a warm smile.

A daffodil sends tender green shoots of leaves above the earth in late winter. If a stone is placed over the bulb, the shoots cannot receive nutrients from the sun, and growth is warped. Negative words are as stones placed on a growing plant. Positive, loving words are like fresh air and sun.

God does not say, "I might love you," or "I love you, but. . . ." God does not seek to control us but surrounds us with affirming and loving freedom. God says, "Yes!" to us: "You are my child, and I love you." If we have been stifled by others much of our lives, we urgently need to hear God's "Yes!" and let it resound in our hearts until joy bursts through.

God wants you to grow, wants to take the stones off your heart. God's word to you is "Yes!" Reply "Yes!" to God, like Mary, simply, purely, with a free heart, that Jesus Christ may be formed within you.

Lord Jesus Christ, you came into the world because of your mother's "Yes!" and defied death with an everlasting "Yes!" Help me grow in love, always affirming you with my "Amen!"

*T*he scene has played itself out repeatedly. The proud father looks at his firstborn son in a room full of family and friends. His heart bursting, he gives his son a precious gift that symbolizes all that he means to him.

The description in John 3 is far different. "For God so loved the world . . ." (v. 16). God does not give the world as a gift to the Son but gives the Son as a gift to the world, a gift that gives salvation, a gift that excuses from condemnation, a gift that brings light.

The unexpected nature of the gift is matched by the unexpected response of human beings: "Light has come into the world, but people loved darkness instead of light" (v. 19).

What a portrait. The God of the universe sends his one and only Son to us, to the human race, in order that we might not be condemned; but people love the darkness instead of the light of God lest their deeds be exposed. Let us live in the truth, for those who live in the truth will embrace the light, living in God's presence without fear. This is good news.

If we walk in the light as he himself is in the light, we have fellowship with one another, and the blood of Jesus his Son cleanses us from all sin.

God, thank you for your matchless gift. Amen.

*I*n November, my sweetheart and I hiked a boardwalk trail through sand dunes at Lake Michigan, and then skipped stones by the shore. We watched children make beachfront castles. The number of grains of sand one can hold in the palm or a shoe is amazing.

God's children outnumber all the grains of sand on all the shores of the world. You are a precious grain of sand in God's palm. God will not let you slip through the fingers.

"God proves his love for us in that while we still were sinners Christ died for us" (v. 8). God sacrificed Jesus, God's very self, for us—a grain of wheat sown in order to bring forth much fruit. God loves you with extreme love. The infant Jesus we celebrate is destined for a harsh death.

Sand cascaded through my palms. Time spent at a beach soothes the soul; we walked back to the car feeling happy and carefree. The next time we get to the beach, half a year will have passed. I wonder what the next months will bring. I hope I will trust God more.

Most loving God, you subjected yourself to death that I might have new life and joy in you. Deepen my trust in Christ, my Savior. Amen.

*T*he Son of God, the one through whom the world was created, the one who knew "that the Father had given all things into his hands" (v. 3), gets up, takes off his outer clothing, grabs a towel, and washes the disciples' feet. Even the twelve who did not understand the fullness of Jesus' identity and mission must have realized that something extraordinary was happening. The one they had followed for these three years was taking the form of a servant with them.

Peter's refusal to go along is natural. Jesus' action seems so out of order. Who wouldn't protest? Peter does more than protest—he all but orders Jesus not to wash his feet. Peter then veers to the other extreme, wanting more than Jesus thinks is necessary.

Our response to Jesus may not be like Peter's, but we can hold out the same hope that Jesus offered: "You do not know now what I am doing, but later you will understand" (v. 7). Lord, help us to understand.

"Cleanse me with hyssop, and I will be clean; wash me, and I will be whiter than snow" (Psalm 51:7).

_W_hat does it mean to abide in God's love in this season?

What did the old painters know
of the place of Jesus' birth?
They thought it insubstantial—
a heap of ruins, a palace in disrepair,
a shelter without safety,
a hovel that was not habitation
but public stage and royal throne.

Perhaps it was the visionary God
who dabbled in their guise to show us
the accessibility of Love:
divinity unguarded reigns
in the lowly kingdom
of the open door.

God our Shelter, we abide in you, and you abide in us. There is no safer place to be. Thank you for the haven of your love; through Jesus, our Friend and Redeemer. Amen.

I have known pastors who sighed over their congregations and people who undermined their pastors. I've seen church members who were not kind and respectful, who used the church to attain power and influence.

I've heard of pastors violating marriage vows and betraying their churches. One friend called her church an alligator because it occasionally chewed up a pastor and spit him out. What people call pastors who betray them, I have no idea.

When church leaders and members forget that the church is the body of Christ and treat each other callously, souls are harmed. We all will give an account to God.

However strained relationships may become in congregations, we are meant to pray for one another and act honorably and with love. We do not do this alone: God upholds the covenant made through Christ, Shepherd of all. Christ prays for us, and the Holy Spirit prays in us that we may become mature in soul, channels for God's love to flood into our lives, washing away the grit of sin, bringing our hearts and the church to joyous flower.

Merciful God, search my heart, and know me. Bring to mind my faults that I may change my ways, and my sin, that I may repent, seek forgiveness, and embrace newness of life through Christ, my Savior and Lord. Amen.

Be subject to one another out of reverence for Christ" (5:21).

At Indiana University, I joined the cave-exploring club and put on old shoes and clothes to crawl around on my belly. The next cave we visited was wondrous: full of beautiful formations with water flowing everywhere. Each of us went at our own pace.

Suddenly, my lamp went out. I called to my companions but could not hear my voice over the roar of mighty waters. I sat on a rock in complete darkness as water rained on me from above and swirled at my feet. The cave floor was a bed of rocks. I could have stumbled had I taken a step. I rested in faith that I would be found.

In minutes, others caught up with me and lit my lamp. They had the foresight to put me, a novice, in the middle of the party.

We are part of a stream of the faithful, those who go before us and know the way and those who come after us who journey the same path. When one of us comes to a standstill, another shows us the way forward.

Blessing comes to all who rest themselves in divine love by night and take bearings from God's wisdom by day. Put on your sneakers, work boots, or fancy shoes, and step out of your comfort zone for God. When you are stuck, others will help you along.

God, may I stand under the stream of your blessing with open hands and receive all that you give through Jesus Christ. Amen.

I sell vintage paper online: old postcards, Victorian trade cards with whimsical images, and scraps. The site I use offers sellers a chance to donate a portion of the proceeds to selected service organizations. The Haitian earthquake spurred me to use this option for the first time. The first fruits of a Victorian gnome scrap will help doctors treat a person in need.

I confess that my impulse on receiving an infrequent paycheck is to splurge on myself: shop for an item of clothing, search an antique mall for ephemera, or buy out-of-season fruit. My financial adviser encourages me to pay myself first by prioritizing saving for retirement as opposed to investing what's left over after expenses have been paid. These practices run counter to stewardship practices suggested by Scripture and the church.

The hard part is recognizing that God gives us everything. My prayers have been answered. God wove replies to my pleas through decades of living. I need to let my gratitude flow out in ways that help others as a first response, not as an afterthought.

God hears your voice. Search the depths of your memory for the answers, and give back to God a portion of gratitude that will bless others.

God, you have been gracious to me in ways I am slow to perceive. Bring to mind your wondrous answers to my prayer, and in response, make me thirst to help others; through Christ our Lord. Amen.